Bake with Dates :

Natural, Healthy, Vegan Recipes Made without Sugar

By

Susan Lowenberg

ISBN-13: 978-1463672898

ISBN-10: 1463672896

Note: Because of the dynamic nature of the Internet, any website addresses or links contained in the book may have changed and may no longer be valid.

Dedication

For my daughter Marissa.

Thank you for your brutally honest opinions and great suggestions.

Table of Contents

Preface

Sugar is poison.

At least for me. I have a sweet tooth, but after eating something with sugar in it I get shaky and cranky. Refined sugar is only empty calories and can lead to malnutrition and disease.

These recipes replace sugar in baked goods like cakes, cookies, pies and quick breads with dates--full of fiber, minerals and vitamins.

All these recipes are vegan, free of all animal products normally found in baked goods-- butter, eggs and milk. These recipes use dates, whole grains and nuts to produce healthy, nutritious food your whole family will enjoy.

About Dates

History

Date palms were one of the earliest cultivated fruit trees. The cultivation of date palms originated in Mesopotamia (now Iraq) about 5,000 years ago. Dates are mentioned in the Bible and the Koran. The "tree of life," date palms provide not only food, but ornamentation, construction material, fiber and fuel. The Moors brought date palm trees to Spain and in turn Spanish missionaries brought date palm seeds to the New World and planted them around their missions in the late 1700s and early 1800s. Most of these missions were in coastal areas and the date palms did not produce high quality fruit due to the cool, humid conditions. Date palms planted by the Spanish missionaries in drier, warmer areas did flourish and provided inspiration for settlers in California and Arizona to cultivate date palms. Many seedling dates were planted in these two states after the Mexican American War and the California Gold Rush.

In the early 1900s the United States Department of Agriculture imported date shoots from Iraq and Egypt and planted them in areas in California, New Mexico and Arizona. When the experiments in California's Coachella Valley showed promise, additional date shoots were imported from Algeria. Today, two California counties, Riverside (which includes the Coachella Valley) and Imperial (which includes the Bard Valley) produce 90% of the dates grown in the United States.

Medjool (an Arabic word whose meaning in unknown) dates are considered the "King of Dates" and are prized for their large size, moist soft flesh, excellent taste, and attractive appearance. All medjool dates originated from a single palm in the Bou Denib Oasis in Saharan Morocco. In the early 1900s disease killed the bulk of the Moroccan medjool date palms. In 1927 eleven offshoots of medjool date palms were imported into the United States by Dr. Walter Swingle. These offshoots were quarantined by being planted in a remote area in Southern Nevada. In 1936, nine of the original eleven offshoots had survived and were relocated to the U.S. Date Garden in Indio, California. In the early 1940s the medjool date palm offshoots were distributed to growers in California and Arizona. Medjool dates are the dominant variety of dates grown in the Bard Valley. Currently 70-75 % of the California date crop is the Deglet Noor variety and 20-25% is the Medjool variety.

Sources: *Imported and American varieties of dates (Phoenix dactylifera) in the United States* by Donald R. Hodel, Dennis V. Johnson, Roy Wesley Nixon. Oakland, CA: ANR Publications, 2007 ; "Date Palm" article in the Food Museum Online website, http://www.foodmuseum.com/datepalm.html

2

Botany

Date palm trees (*Phoenix dactylifera*) thrive with "their feet in water and their heads in the sun." Since they need plenty of water and high heat to produce fruit, date palms grow best in hot arid climates, where the underground water supply is plentiful.

Date palms can live 100 years or more and grown up to 100 feet in that time. Date palm trees grow 12 to 18 inches in diameter. The tree is dioecious, meaning there are female and male plants. Flowers are borne in bunches at the top of the tree. Only female trees produce fruit, but one male tree can produce enough pollen to pollinate 40-50 female trees. A date palm tree starts producing fruit in 3 to 5 years and is fully mature in 12 years. One mature female tree produces 150-200 pounds of fruit annually.

Sources: *Imported and American varieties of dates (Phoenix dactylifera) in the United States* by Donald R. Hodel, Dennis V. Johnson, Roy Wesley Nixon. Oakland, CA: ANR Publications, 2007 ; "Date Palm" article in the Food Museum Online website, http://www.foodmuseum.com/datepalm.html ; "The Date, Phoenix Dactylifera" by P. Gepts, http://www.plantsciences.ucdavis.edu/gepts/pb143/CROP/Date/Date.htm

Nutritional Value

Dates are considered an ideal food, with a wide range of essential nutrients and many health benefits.

Dates are high in fiber and help promote a healthy digestive system. Dates are an excellent source of potassium, a nutrient needed to maintain a healthy nervous system. Dates contain many vitamins like A, B1, B2 and nicotinic acid (niacin) that help maintain a healthy body by metabolizing carbohydrates and maintaining blood glucose levels. Dates have higher percentages of potassium, phosphorous and iron than other fruits. Dates also contain a higher percentage of protein than other fruits. Dates are free of fat and cholesterol and are low in sodium.

Although dates have high sugar content--approximately 70-80% in the form of glucose, fructose and sucrose--dates have a low glycemic index. The consumption of dates will not result in rapid and large fluctuations in blood sugar levels.

Bedouin Arabs, who eat dates on a regular basis, have extremely low rates of cancer and heart disease.

Dietary guidelines recommend eating foods low in sodium, fat and cholesterol and high in fiber. Dates perfectly fulfill these recommendations.

Sources: "Biochemical and Nutritional Characterizations of Date Palm Fruits (Phoenix dactylifera L.)" by El-Sohaimy S.A. and Hafez E.E. Journal of Applied Sciences Research (2010) 6(8):1060-1067 ; "The Glycaemic Index of Dates and Date/Yoghurt Mixed Meals. Are Dates 'the Candy that Grows on Trees'?" by CJ Miller, EV Dunn and IB Hashim. European Journal of Clinical Nutrition (2003) 57:427-430 ; "The

Fruit of the Date Palm: Its Possible Use as the Best Food for the Future?" by Walid Al-Shahib and Richard J. Marshall. International Journal of Food Sciences and Nutrition (July 2003) 54(4):247-259.

Buying and storing

When purchasing, choose dates that are moist, plump and dark brown, with a shiny skin. Avoid shriveled dates or those with mold or sugar crystals on the skin.

Store dates in an airtight container at room temperature. Dates may be stored for six months to a year.

Use

Pit dates by cutting lengthwise and pulling out the pit. Slice date lengthwise twice more and then chop each slice three or four times.

Cut out any hard brown scars on the dates. If the date is black inside do not use it.

When using in recipes with almond milk, combine chopped dates in the almond milk for several minutes to soften before blending.

If dates are dry and hard, soak them in water for a few minutes. Drain water from dates before adding to other ingredients in the recipe.

In these recipes, dates are placed in a blender with sour almond milk or almond milk and other liquid ingredients and blended until pureed.

Other Ingredients

Almond milk

The almond milk used in all recipes is Almond Breeze Unsweetened, with no added sugar. Either the vanilla or the original unsweetened varieties may be used. Unsweetened almond milk has only 40 calories per cup and has a low glycemic index.

Sour almond milk

Sour almond milk is used as an egg substitute in these recipes. Sour almond milk helps make the baked goods tender and moist.

To make 1 cup sour almond milk, simply put 1 T. apple cider vinegar in a measuring cup and add almond milk to make 1 cup total liquid.

Use 1 1/2 tsp. apple cider vinegar for 1/2 cup sour almond milk.

Use 3/4 tsp. apple cider vinegar for 1/4 cup sour almond milk.

Almond Meal

Almond meal, also called almond flour, is simply raw almonds finely ground. Used to replace some of the flour in the recipes, almond meal adds protein, as well as vitamins and minerals.

Almonds are technically a seed, rather than a nut. "Almonds are high in monounsaturated fats, the same type of health-promoting fats as are found in olive oil, which have been associated with reduced risk of heart disease," by lowering cholesterol. Almonds are also high in Vitamin E, magnesium and potassium.

"Almonds appear to not only decrease after-meal rises in blood sugar, but also provide antioxidants to mop up the smaller amounts of free radicals that still result. . . . Further research shows that eating almonds along with a high glycemic index food significantly lowers the glycemic index of the meal and lessens the rise in blood sugar after eating."

Do not purchase blanched almond flour as it is the whole almond, with the skin, that provides the most nutrition. "The flavonoids found in almond skins team up with the vitamin E found in their meat to more than double the antioxidant punch either delivers when administered separately, shows a study published in the *Journal of Nutrition*."

Source: "Almonds" in The World's Healthiest Foods website,
http://whfoods.org/genpage.php?tname=foodspice&dbid=20

Carob Powder

Carob has no caffeine, which is the reason I prefer it. Carob is also high in fiber, is high in antioxidants and contains vitamins A, B, B2, B3 and D.

If you want to make chocolate baked goods instead of carob, simply substitute an equal amount of cocoa powder for the carob powder in each recipe.

Source: "What Are the Health Benefits of Carob" article by Franchesca Vermillion on the Livestrong website, http://www.livestrong.com/article/410419-what-are-the-health-benefits-of-carob/

Applesauce

Individual 3.9 oz (111g) containers of Mott's Natural applesauce with no added sugar were used in these recipes. These individual 1/2 cup containers are a perfect, convenient size for baking. These packages keep well in the pantry and there is no spoilage, which happens when an open container of applesauce is left in the refrigerator.

Walnuts

Walnuts benefit the heart and circulatory system by decreasing LDL and total cholesterol, decreasing the risk of excess blood clotting and decreasing the risk of excessive inflammation.

Walnuts "are a rich source of heart-healthy monounsaturated fats and an excellent source of those hard to find omega-3 fatty acids." ". . . walnuts are unique in their collection of anti-inflammatory nutrients. These nutrients include omega-3 fatty acids; phytonutrients including tannins, phenolic acids, and flavonoids; quinones like juglone; and other anti-inflammatory phytonutrients."

Source: "Walnuts" in The World's Healthiest Foods website, http://whfoods.org/genpage.php?tname=foodspice&dbid=99

Apple Coffee Cake

6		medjool dates, pitted and chopped
1/2	cup	sour almond milk
1/2	cup	almond milk
1/2	cup	applesauce
1	tsp	vanilla
1	cup	whole wheat flour
1/2	cup	almond meal
1	Tbs	baking powder
2	tsp	cinnamon

1/2	tsp	salt
2		apples, peeled, cored and shredded

Nut Topping

1/2	cup	chopped walnuts
1/2	cup	almond meal
1/2	cup	date syrup (p. 79)
1	tsp	cinnamon

Procedure

1 Using a blender, puree dates, sour almond milk, almond milk, applesauce and vanilla.

2 Combine flour, 1/2 cup almond meal, baking powder, 2 tsp. cinnamon and salt.

3 Add date mixture to dry ingredients and stir until combined. Gently fold in shredded apples.

4 For nut topping, combine walnuts, 1/2 cup almond meal, date syrup and 1 tsp. cinnamon in small bowl and mix well.

5 Spray 8" square pan with cooking spray. Spread batter into pan. Drop nut topping evenly over the batter.

6 Bake at 350° F for 50 minutes.

Servings: 9

Oven Temperature: 350°F

Preparation Time: 20 minutes
Cooking Time: 50 minutes

Nutrition Facts

Serving size: 1 slice.

Amount Per Serving	
Calories	219.47
Calories From Fat (27%)	58.37
	% Daily Value
Total Fat 6.86g	11%
Saturated Fat 0.56g	3%
Cholesterol 0mg	0%
Sodium 313.08mg	13%
Potassium 290.95mg	8%
Total Carbohydrates 38.73g	13%
Fiber 4.09g	16%
Sugar 22.31g	
Protein 4.09g	8%

Banana Cake

12		medjool dates, pitted and chopped	1 1/2	tsp	baking powder
1 2/3	cups	sour almond milk	1	tsp	baking soda
1	tsp	vanilla	1/2	tsp	salt
2	cups	whole wheat flour	3		medium ripe bananas
1/2	cup	almond meal			

Procedure

1 Combine flour, almond meal, baking powder, baking soda and salt.

2 Using a blender, puree dates, sour almond milk, and vanilla. Add bananas and puree lightly.

3 Add date/banana mixture to dry ingredients and stir until combined.

4 Pour batter into 8" x 11.5" x 2" baking dish.

5 Bake at 350° F for 30-35 minutes.

6 Frost with Banana Frosting (p.9) or Tangy Nut Frosting (p.18) when cooled to touch.

Servings: 12

Oven Temperature: 350°F

Preparation Time: 15 minutes
Cooking Time: 35 minutes

Nutrition Facts

Serving size: 1 slice.

Amount Per Serving	
Calories	184.44
Calories From Fat (7%)	13.49
	% Daily Value
Total Fat 1.57g	2%
Saturated Fat 0.12g	<1%
Cholesterol 0mg	0%
Sodium 288.71mg	12%
Potassium 321.98mg	9%
Total Carbohydrates 41.36g	14%
Fiber 3.23g	13%
Sugar 19.71g	
Protein 3.4g	7%

Banana Frosting

1/2 cup date syrup (p. 79)
1/2 cup almond meal

1   ripe banana, mashed

Procedure

1 Mix in small bowl until well combined.

Servings: 12

Preparation Time: 5 minutes

Nutrition Facts

Serving size: 1/12 of a recipe (1 ounce).

Amount Per Serving	
Calories	40.25
Calories From Fat (17%)	7.01
	% Daily Value
Total Fat 0.79g	1%
Saturated Fat 0.06g	<1%
Cholesterol 0mg	0%
Sodium 0.39mg	<1%
Potassium 91.12mg	3%
Total Carbohydrates 8.51g	3%
Fiber 0.94g	4%
Sugar 6.59g	
Protein 0.6g	1%

Blueberry Coffee Cake

6		medjool dates, pitted and chopped	1/2	tsp	salt
1/2	cup	sour almond milk	12	oz	frozen blueberries
1/2	cup	almond milk	**Nut Topping**		
1	tsp	vanilla	1/2	cup	chopped walnuts
1	cup	whole wheat flour	1/2	cup	almond meal
1/2	cup	almond meal	1/2	cup	date syrup (p. 79)
1	Tbs	baking powder	1	tsp	cinnamon
1	tsp	cinnamon			

Procedure

1 Using a blender, puree dates, sour almond milk, almond milk, and vanilla.

2 Combine flour, 1/2 cup almond meal, baking powder, 1 tsp. cinnamon and salt.

3 Add date mixture to flour mixture and stir until combined. Gently fold in blueberries.

4 To make nut topping, combine walnuts, 1/2 cup almond meal, date syrup and 1 tsp. cinnamon in small bowl and mix well.

5 Spray 8" square pan with cooking spray. Spread batter into pan. Drop nut topping evenly over the batter.

6 Bake at 350º F for 50-55 minutes.

Servings: 9

Oven Temperature: 350°F

Preparation Time: 15 minutes
Cooking Time: 55 minutes

Nutrition Facts

Serving size: 1 piece.

Amount Per Serving	
Calories	220.95
Calories From Fat (27%)	58.95
	% Daily Value
Total Fat 6.94g	11%
Saturated Fat 0.57g	3%
Cholesterol 0mg	0%
Sodium 313.16mg	13%
Potassium 283.18mg	8%
Total Carbohydrates 38.82g	13%
Fiber 4.33g	17%
Sugar 21.92g	
Protein 4.26g	9%

Carob Cake

12		medjool dates, pitted and chopped	1	cup	almond meal
1 1/2	cup	sour almond milk	1/2	cup	carob powder
1/2	cup	applesauce	2	tsp	baking soda
1	tsp	vanilla	1/2	tsp	salt
1	cup	whole wheat flour			Carob Nut Cream (p. 12)

Procedure

1 Using a blender, puree dates, sour almond milk, applesauce and vanilla.

2 Combine flour, almond meal, carob powder, baking soda and salt.

3 Add date mixture to dry ingredients and stir until combined.

4 Pour batter into 8" x 11.5" x 2" pan.

5 Bake at 350° F for 30-35 minutes.

6 Frost with Carob Nut Cream (p. 12) when cooled to touch.

Servings: 12

Oven Temperature: 350°F

Preparation Time: 15 minutes
Cooking Time: 35 minutes

Nutrition Facts

Serving size: 1 piece.

Amount Per Serving	
Calories	227.36
Calories From Fat (23%)	52.07
	% Daily Value
Total Fat 6.15g	9%
Saturated Fat 0.42g	2%
Cholesterol 0mg	0%
Sodium 337.83mg	14%
Potassium 348.63mg	10%
Total Carbohydrates 41.86g	14%
Fiber 5.77g	23%
Sugar 26.16g	
Protein 4.27g	9%

Carob Nut Cream

1 cup nuts	1/4 cup carob powder
1/4 cup almond milk	1 tsp alcohol-free vanilla
2/3 cup date syrup (p. 79)	

Procedure

1 In food processor, finely grind nuts.

2 Add almond milk, date syrup, carob powder and vanilla and process until smooth.

Servings: 12
Yield: 1 3/4 cups

Nutrition Facts

Serving size: 1 ounce.

Amount Per Serving	
Calories	81.35
Calories From Fat (42%)	33.93
	% Daily Value
Total Fat 4.06g	6%
Saturated Fat 0.3g	2%
Cholesterol 0mg	0%
Sodium 7.99mg	<1%
Potassium 138.63mg	4%
Total Carbohydrates 10.64g	4%
Fiber 2.01g	8%
Sugar 7.75g	
Protein 1.92g	4%

Recipe Tips

Use raw, unsalted almonds, cashews, macadamia nuts, pecans, or walnuts.

If you don't have date syrup on hand, substitute 9 chopped dates and increase almond milk to 2/3 cup.

Carrot Cake

6		medjool dates, pitted and chopped		1/3	cup	chopped walnuts
1/2	cups	sour almond milk		8	oz	can crushed pineapple, undrained
1/2	cups	applesauce		2	cups	grated carrot, packed
1	tsp	vanilla		**Nut Topping**		
1	cups	whole wheat flour		1/2	cup	chopped walnuts
1/2	cup	almond meal		1/2	cup	almond meal
1	Tbs	baking powder		1/2	cup	date syrup (p. 79)
1	tsp	cinnamon		1	tsp	cinnamon
1/2	tsp	salt				

Procedure

1 Using a blender, puree dates, sour almond milk, applesauce and vanilla.

2 Combine flour, 1/2 cup almond meal, baking powder, 1 tsp. cinnamon, salt and 1/3 cup chopped walnuts.

3 Add date mixture to flour mixture and stir until combined. Fold in crushed pineapple and carrots.

4 Spray 8" square pan with cooking spray and pour cake batter into pan.

5 To make topping, combine 1/2 cup walnuts, 1/2 cup almond meal, date syrup and 1 tsp. cinnamon in small bowl and mix well. Drop nut topping evenly over the cake batter.

6 Bake at 350° F for 50 minutes.

Servings: 9

Oven Temperature: 350°F

Preparation Time: 20 minutes
Cooking Time: 50 minutes

Nutrition Facts

Serving size: 1 piece.

Amount Per Serving	
Calories	256.03
Calories From Fat (32%)	80.7
	% Daily Value
Total Fat 9.53g	15%
Saturated Fat 0.83g	4%
Cholesterol 0mg	0%
Sodium 321.49mg	13%
Potassium 381.35mg	11%
Total Carbohydrates 41.51g	14%
Fiber 4.54g	18%
Sugar 24.34g	
Protein 4.94g	10%

Variation

Omit the Nut Topping and frost with Tangy Nut Frosting (p. 18) when cake is cool.

Cinnamon Coffee Cake

6		medjool dates, pitted and chopped	1/2	tsp	salt
1	cup	sour almond milk	**Nut Topping**		
1/2	cup	applesauce	1	cup	chopped walnuts
1	tsp	vanilla	1	cup	almond meal
1	cup	whole wheat flour	1	cup	date syrup (p. 79)
1/2	cup	almond meal	2	tsp	cinnamon
1	Tbs	baking powder			
2	tsp	cinnamon			

Procedure

1 Using a blender, puree dates, sour almond milk, applesauce and vanilla.

2 Combine flour, 1/2 cup almond meal, baking powder, 2 tsp. cinnamon and salt.

3 Add date mixture to flour mixture and stir until combined.

4 To make topping, combine walnuts, 1 cup almond meal, date syrup and 2 tsp. cinnamon in small bowl and mix well.

5 Spray 8" square pan with cooking spray.

6 Spread half of the batter into pan. Drop half of the topping evenly over the batter. Spread the remainder of the batter into pan. Take a knife and swirl nut topping into batter. Drop remainder of nut topping evenly onto cake.

7 Bake at 350° F for 20-25 minutes.

Servings: 9

Oven Temperature: 350°F

Preparation Time: 15 minutes
Cooking Time: 25 minutes

Nutrition Facts

Serving size: 1 piece.

Amount Per Serving	
Calories	290.36
Calories From Fat (35%)	102.51
	% Daily Value
Total Fat 12.08g	19%
Saturated Fat 1.02g	5%
Cholesterol 0mg	0%
Sodium 316.09mg	13%
Potassium 369.27mg	11%
Total Carbohydrates 44.29g	15%
Fiber 4.94g	20%
Sugar 26.78g	
Protein 5.67g	11%

Double Date Cake

12		medjool dates, pitted and chopped
1	cup	boiling water
6		medjool dates, pitted and chopped
1	cup	sour almond milk
1	tsp	vanilla
1/2	cup	whole wheat flour
1/2	cup	almond meal

1	tsp	baking soda
1/3	cup	chopped pecans

Date Frosting

12		medjool dates, pitted and chopped
1/2	cup	water

Procedure

1 Pour 1 cup boiling water over 12 chopped dates.

2 Using a blender, puree 6 chopped dates, sour almond milk and vanilla.

3 Combine flour, almond meal, baking soda and pecans.

4 Stir pureed date mixture into flour mixture until well combined.

5 Drain soaked dates and fold into batter.

6 Spray 8" square pan with cooking spray. Pour batter into pan.

7 Bake at 350° F for 30 minutes.

8 To make date frosting, combine 12 chopped dates and 1/2 cup water in medium saucepan. Bring to a boil, reduce heat and simmer until thick, about 10 minutes. Cool.

9 When cake is cool to the touch, top with date frosting.

Servings: 12

Oven Temperature: 350°F

Preparation Time: 20 minutes
Cooking Time: 30 minutes

Nutrition Facts

Serving size: 1 piece.

Amount Per Serving	
Calories	219.42
Calories From Fat (13%)	28.48
	% Daily Value
Total Fat 3.36g	5%
Saturated Fat 0.25g	1%
Cholesterol 0mg	0%
Sodium 121.5mg	5%
Potassium 452.23mg	13%
Total Carbohydrates 49.84g	17%
Fiber 4.68g	19%
Sugar 40.11g	
Protein 2.34g	5%

Nut Cream

1	cup	nuts	2/3	cup	date syrup (p. 79)
1/4	cup	almond milk	1	tsp	alcohol-free vanilla

Procedure

1 In food processor, finely grind nuts.

2 Add almond milk, date syrup and vanilla and process until smooth.

Servings: 12
Yield: 1 1/2 cups

Nutrition Facts

Serving size: 2 oz.

Amount Per Serving	
Calories	78.02
Calories From Fat (43%)	33.93
	% Daily Value
Total Fat 4.06g	6%
Saturated Fat 0.3g	2%
Cholesterol 0mg	0%
Sodium 7.99mg	<1%
Potassium 138.63mg	4%
Total Carbohydrates 9.81g	3%
Fiber 1.67g	7%
Sugar 7.42g	
Protein 1.92g	4%

Recipe Tips

Use raw, unsalted almonds, cashews, macadamia nuts, pecans, or walnuts.

If you don't have date syrup on hand, substitute 9 chopped dates and increase almond milk to 2/3 cup.

Orange Date Coffee Cake

12		medjool dates, pitted and chopped, divided
1/2	cup	sour almond milk
1/2	cup	applesauce
1/2	cup	orange juice
1	tsp	vanilla
1	cup	whole wheat flour
1/2	cup	almond meal
1	Tbs	baking powder
1/2	tsp	salt
1	Tbs	finely shredded orange peel

Nut Topping

1/2	cup	chopped walnuts
1/2	cup	almond meal
1/2	cup	date syrup (p. 79)
1	tsp	cinnamon

Procedure

3 Using a blender, puree 6 chopped dates, sour almond milk, applesauce, orange juice and vanilla.

4 Combine flour, ½ cup almond meal, baking powder, salt and orange peel.

5 Drop 6 chopped dates into flour mixture one at a time, stirring to coat each piece with flour so the date pieces won't clump together.

6 Add blended date mixture to flour mixture and stir until combined.

7 To make topping, combine walnuts, 1/2 cup almond meal, date syrup and cinnamon in small bowl and mix well.

8 Spray 8" square pan with cooking spray. Spread batter into pan. Drop nut topping evenly over the batter.

9 Bake at 350° F for 20-25 minutes.

Servings: 9

Oven Temperature: 350°F

Preparation Time: 15 minutes
Cooking Time: 25 minutes

Nutrition Facts

Serving size: 1 piece.

Amount Per Serving	
Calories	253.33
Calories From Fat (22%)	56.83
	% Daily Value
Total Fat 6.68g	10%
Saturated Fat 0.56g	3%
Cholesterol 0mg	0%
Sodium 303.34mg	13%
Potassium 392.63mg	11%
Total Carbohydrates 48.12g	16%
Fiber 4.53g	18%
Sugar 31.22g	
Protein 4.33g	9%

Tangy Nut Frosting

9	medjool dates, pitted and chopped	2	tsp	fresh lemon juice
2/3	cup almond milk	1/2	cup	almond meal

Procedure

1 Using a blender, puree dates, almond milk, and lemon juice. Transfer date mixture to small bowl. Stir almond meal into date mixture until smooth.

Servings: 12

Preparation Time: 5 minutes

Nutrition Facts

Serving size: 1/12 of a recipe (1.3 ounces).

Amount Per Serving	
Calories	61.27
Calories From Fat (14%)	8.49
	% Daily Value
Total Fat 0.97g	1%
Saturated Fat 0.05g	<1%
Cholesterol 0mg	0%
Sodium 10.19mg	<1%
Potassium 136.71mg	4%
Total Carbohydrates 13.91g	5%
Fiber 1.41g	6%
Sugar 12.04g	
Protein 0.73g	1%

Almond Cookies

12		medjool dates, pitted and chopped	1 3/4	cups	whole wheat flour
1/2	cup	sour almond milk	1 1/3	cups	almond meal
1/3	cup	almond milk	1/2	tsp	baking soda
1	tsp	almond extract	36		Whole almonds

Procedure

1 Using a blender, puree dates, sour almond milk, almond milk, and almond extract.

2 Combine flour, almond meal and baking soda.

3 Stir date mixture into dry ingredients until combined.

4 Form the dough into 2 rolls or logs that are 10 to 12 inches long. Wrap and refrigerate for 2 hours.

5 Take a log and cut the dough at 1/2" intervals. Place slices of dough on a baking sheet lined with parchment paper about an inch apart and press them down slightly, shaping them into round cookies.

6 Place a whole almond on to the top of each cookie and lightly press it into place, then paint the surface of the cookie with some almond milk using a pastry brush.

7 Bake at 325º F for 13-15 minutes.

Servings: 36
Yield: 36 cookies

Oven Temperature: 325°F

Preparation Time: 50 minutes
Cooking Time: 15 minutes

Nutrition Facts

Serving size: 1 cookie.

Amount Per Serving	
Calories	60.28
Calories From Fat (20%)	12.18
	% Daily Value
Total Fat 1.41g	2%
Saturated Fat 0.1g	<1%
Cholesterol 0mg	0%
Sodium 21.86mg	<1%
Potassium 75.04mg	2%
Total Carbohydrates 11.16g	4%
Fiber 1g	4%
Sugar 5.43g	
Protein 1.36g	3%

Blondies

12		medjool dates, pitted and chopped	1/2	cup	almond meal
1 1/2	cup	sour almond milk	2	tsp	baking powder
1/2	cup	roasted almond butter	1/2	tsp	salt
1	tsp	vanilla	1/3	cup	chopped pecans
1 1/2	cups	whole wheat flour			

Procedure

1 Using a blender, puree dates, sour almond milk, almond butter, and vanilla.

2 Combine flour, almond meal, baking powder, salt and pecans.

3 Stir date mixture into dry ingredients until combined.

4 Spray 9" x 13" baking pan with cooking spray. Spread batter into pan.

5 Bake at 350° F for 20-25 minutes.

Servings: 24

Oven Temperature: 350°F

Preparation Time: 15 minutes
Cooking Time: 25 minutes

Nutrition Facts

Serving size: 1 blondie.

Amount Per Serving	
Calories	111.82
Calories From Fat (35%)	39.24
	% Daily Value
Total Fat 4.67g	7%
Saturated Fat 0.35g	2%
Cholesterol 0mg	0%
Sodium 100.99mg	4%
Potassium 149.27mg	4%
Total Carbohydrates 16.53g	6%
Fiber 1.83g	7%
Sugar 8.34g	
Protein 2.49g	5%

Blueberry Oatmeal Bars

Filling

12	oz	fresh or frozen blueberries
1/4	cup	date syrup (p. 79)
1	Tbs	cornstarch

Crust

12		medjool dates, pitted and chopped

3/4	cup	sour almond milk
1 3/4	cups	rolled oats
1	cups	whole wheat flour
1/2	cup	almond meal
1	tsp	baking soda
1/2	tsp	salt

Procedure

To Make the Filling

1 Mix date syrup and cornstarch together until well blended.

2 Place blueberries in saucepan and stir in date/cornstarch mixture.

3 Bring to a boil, then reduce heat and simmer until blueberries release their juices and the mixture is thick, about 5-10 minutes. Cool.

To Make the Crust

1 Using a blender, puree dates and sour almond milk.

2 Combine rolled oats, flour, almond meal, baking soda and salt.

3 Stir date mixture into oat mixture until well combined.

To Make the Bars

1 Spray 8" square pan with cooking spray.

2 Spread half the crust mixture into pan, pressing down well.

3 Spread filling on top of crust. Add remaining crust mixture, pressing down well.

4 Bake at 350° F for 30 minutes.

Servings: 16

Oven Temperature: 350°F

Preparation Time: 20 minutes
Cooking Time: 30 minutes

Nutrition Facts

Serving size: 1 bar.

Amount Per Serving	
Calories	175.76
Calories From Fat (10%)	17.64
	% Daily Value
Total Fat 2.08g	3%
Saturated Fat 0.26g	1%
Cholesterol 0mg	0%
Sodium 160.82mg	7%
Potassium 253.11mg	7%
Total Carbohydrates 36.83g	12%
Fiber 4.09g	16%
Sugar 16.14g	
Protein 4.54g	9%

Carob Brownies

18		medjool dates, pitted and chopped	1/3	cup	carob powder
1	cup	sour almond milk	1	tsp	baking powder
1	tsp	vanilla	1/2	tsp	salt
3/4	cup	whole wheat flour	1/3	cup	chopped walnuts

Procedure

1 Using a blender, puree dates, sour almond milk, and vanilla.

2 Combine flour, carob powder, baking powder, salt and walnuts.

3 Stir date mixture into dry ingredients until combined.

4 Spray 8" square pan with cooking spray. Spread dough into pan.

5 Bake at 350° F for 25-30 minutes.

Servings: 12

Oven Temperature: 350°F

Preparation Time: 15 minutes
Cooking Time: 30 minutes

Nutrition Facts

Serving size: 1 brownie.

Amount Per Serving	
Calories	162.76
Calories From Fat (13%)	21.23
	% Daily Value
Total Fat 2.54g	4%
Saturated Fat 0.21g	1%
Cholesterol 0mg	0%
Sodium 153.14mg	6%
Potassium 289.7mg	8%
Total Carbohydrates 35.91g	12%
Fiber 3.81g	15%
Sugar 24.96g	
Protein 2.04g	4%

Carob Chip Cookies

12		medjool dates, pitted and chopped	1/2	cup	almond meal
1	cup	sour almond milk	1	tsp	baking soda
1		banana	1/2	tsp	salt
1 1/2	tsp	vanilla	2	cups	carob chips (p. 24)
2	cups	whole wheat flour			

Procedure

1 Combine flour, almond meal, baking soda and salt.

2 Using a blender, puree dates, sour almond milk, banana and vanilla.

3 Combine date mixture with flour mixture. Gently fold in carob chips.

4 Use two spoons to drop batter onto baking sheet lined with parchment paper.

5 Bake at 350° F for 12 minutes.

Servings: 44
Yield: 44 cookies

Oven Temperature: 350°F

Preparation Time: 30 minutes
Cooking Time: 12 minutes

Nutrition Facts

Serving size: 1 cookie.

Amount Per Serving	
Calories	48.28
Calories From Fat (12%)	5.82
	% Daily Value
Total Fat 0.68g	1%
Saturated Fat 0.3g	2%
Cholesterol 0mg	0%
Sodium 59.34mg	2%
Potassium 66.27mg	2%
Total Carbohydrates 10.12g	3%
Fiber 0.76g	3%
Sugar 4.81g	
Protein 0.85g	2%

Carob Chips

Use refined coconut oil, not virgin coconut oil. Virgin coconut oil has a strong taste of coconut, which does not work in this recipe.

1/2	cup	refined coconut oil		2	Tbs	date syrup (p. 79)
6	Tbs	carob powder		1 1/2	tsp	alcohol-free vanilla

Procedure

1 Melt coconut oil in microwave for 1 minute. Blend all ingredients until smooth.

2 Spread carob mixture in a thin layer in a 9" x 13" glass baking dish greased with coconut oil. Refrigerate for one hour.

3 When hardened, cut into chips. Store chips in an airtight container in the refrigerator.

Servings: 8
Yield: 2 cups.

Preparation Time: 15 minutes

Nutrition Facts

Serving size: 1/8 of a recipe (0.8 ounces).

Amount Per Serving	
Calories	145.3
Calories From Fat (83%)	120
	% Daily Value
Total Fat 14g	22%
Saturated Fat 12g	60%
Cholesterol 0mg	0%
Sodium 0.14mg	<1%
Potassium 21.74mg	<1%
Total Carbohydrates 6.02g	2%
Fiber 1.69g	7%
Sugar 3.5g	
Protein 0.05g	<1%

Carob Oat Cookies

12		medjool dates, pitted and chopped	1	cup	whole wheat flour
1/2	cup	sour almond milk	1/4	cup	carob powder
2		bananas	1	tsp	baking soda
1	tsp	vanilla	1/2	cup	chopped walnuts
1	cup	rolled oats			

Procedure

1 Combine rolled oats, flour, carob powder baking soda and walnuts.

2 Using a blender, puree dates, sour almond milk, bananas and vanilla.

3 Mix date mixture into flour mixture.

4 Use two spoons to drop batter onto baking sheet lined with parchment paper.

5 Bake at 350° F for 12 minutes.

Servings: 36
Yield: 36 cookies

Oven Temperature: 350°F

Preparation Time: 30 minutes
Cooking Time: 12 minutes

Nutrition Facts

Serving size: 1 cookie.

Amount Per Serving	
Calories	71.23
Calories From Fat (17%)	12.33
	% Daily Value
Total Fat 1.48g	2%
Saturated Fat 0.17g	<1%
Cholesterol 0mg	0%
Sodium 37.8mg	2%
Potassium 111.43mg	3%
Total Carbohydrates 13.84g	5%
Fiber 1.6g	6%
Sugar 6.41g	
Protein 1.57g	3%

Cinnamon Cookies

18		medjool dates, pitted and chopped	1	Tbs	ground cinnamon
1	cup	sour almond milk	2	tsp	baking soda
1	tsp	vanilla	1/2	tsp	salt
2 1/4	cup	whole wheat flour	4	Tbs	date sugar
1/2	cup	almond meal	1	Tbs	ground cinnamon

Procedure

1 Using a blender, puree dates, sour almond milk, and vanilla.

2 Combine flour, almond meal, 1 T. cinnamon, baking soda and salt.

3 Stir date mixture into dry ingredients.

4 Combine date sugar and 1 T. ground cinnamon in small bowl.

5 Roll dough into 1 inch balls. Roll cookie balls in cinnamon/date sugar mixture. Place balls on baking sheet lined with parchment paper. Flatten cookies with bottom of a glass.

6 Bake at 350º F for 10-12 minutes.

Servings: 42
Yield: 42 cookies

Oven Temperature: 350°F

Preparation Time: 30 minutes
Cooking Time: 10 minutes

Nutrition Facts

Serving size: 1 cookie.

Amount Per Serving	
Calories	62.45
Calories From Fat (5%)	3.3
	% Daily Value
Total Fat 0.38g	<1%
Saturated Fat 0.03g	<1%
Cholesterol 0mg	0%
Sodium 92.18mg	4%
Potassium 85.03mg	2%
Total Carbohydrates 14.68g	5%
Fiber 1.28g	5%
Sugar 8.03g	
Protein 1.02g	2%

Note

Date sugar is low moisture dates that have been dried and ground fine. The ground dates are often mixed with oat flour to prevent the date granules sticking together. Date sugar may be purchased from a health food store.

Cranberry Oatmeal Bars

Filling

12	oz	fresh or frozen cranberries
1/2	cup	date syrup (p. 79)

Crust

12		medjool dates, pitted and chopped
3/4	cup	sour almond milk

1 3/4	cups	rolled oats
1	cups	whole wheat flour
1/2	cup	almond meal
1	tsp	baking soda
1/2	tsp	salt

Procedure

To Make the Filling

1 Combine cranberries and date syrup in medium saucepan and bring to a boil.

2 Reduce heat and cook until cranberries pop, about 10 minutes. Cool.

To Make the Crust

1 Using a blender, puree dates and sour almond milk.

2 Combine rolled oats, flour, almond meal, baking soda and salt.

3 Stir date mixture into oat mixture until combined.

To Make the Bars

1 Spray 8" square pan with cooking spray.

2 Spread half the crust mixture into pan, pressing down well.

3 Spread filling on top of crust. Add remaining crust mixture, pressing down well.

4 Bake at 350° F for 30 minutes.

Servings: 16

Oven Temperature: 350°F

Preparation Time: 20 minutes
Cooking Time: 30 minutes

Nutrition Facts

Serving size: 1 bar.

Amount Per Serving	
Calories	166.48
Calories From Fat (10%)	17.16
	% Daily Value
Total Fat 2.02g	3%
Saturated Fat 0.26g	1%
Cholesterol 0mg	0%
Sodium 160.76mg	7%
Potassium 245.49mg	7%
Total Carbohydrates 34.55g	12%
Fiber 4.05g	16%
Sugar 14.44g	
Protein 4.42g	9%

Cut-Out Cookies

12		medjool dates, pitted and chopped	1	cup	almond meal
1	cup	sour almond milk	1/2	tsp	baking soda
1	tsp	vanilla	1/2	tsp	salt
2	cups	whole wheat flour			

Procedure

1 Using a blender, puree dates, sour almond milk and vanilla.

2 Combine flour, almond meal, baking soda and salt.

3 Stir date mixture into dry ingredients. Knead dough 4-5 times in bowl, until all the flour is incorporated.

4 Work with half of the dough at a time. Roll dough between pieces of plastic wrap to 1/8" thickness. Cut into desired shapes.

5 Bake at 350° F for 10 minutes.

Servings: 48
Yield: 48 cookies

Oven Temperature: 350°F

Preparation Time: 1 hour
Cooking Time: 10 minutes

Nutrition Facts

Serving size: 1 cookie.

Amount Per Serving	
Calories	49.5
Calories From Fat (21%)	10.46
	% Daily Value
Total Fat 1.24g	2%
Saturated Fat 0.03g	<1%
Cholesterol 0mg	0%
Sodium 78.76mg	3%
Potassium 91.01mg	3%
Total Carbohydrates 9.07g	3%
Fiber 0.85g	3%
Sugar 4.04g	
Protein 1.05g	2%

Recipe Tips

Serving suggestions: top with all fruit spread; make Linzer cookies and spread the bottom half with all fruit spread; frost with Nut Cream (p. 16) or Carob Nut Cream (p.12); decorate with dried fruit before baking; eat as is.

Date Oatmeal Bars

Filling

14		medjool dates, pitted and chopped
1/2	cup	water
1/2	cup	chopped pecans

Crust

12		medjool dates, pitted and chopped
3/4	cup	sour almond milk
1 3/4	cups	rolled oats
1	cups	whole wheat flour
1/2	cup	almond meal
1	tsp	baking soda
1/2	tsp	salt

Procedure

To Make the Filling

1 Bring 14 chopped dates and water to a boil, reduce heat and simmer until thick.

2 Cool. Stir in pecans.

To Make the Crust

1 Using a blender, puree 12 chopped dates and sour almond milk.

2 Combine rolled oats, flour, almond meal, baking soda and salt.

3 Stir date mixture into oat mixture until combined.

To Make the Bars

1 Spray 8" square pan with cooking spray.

2 Spread half the crust mixture into pan, pressing down well.

3 Spread filling on top of crust. Add remaining crust mixture, pressing down well.

4 Bake at 350º F for 30 minutes.

Servings: 16

Oven Temperature: 350°F

Preparation Time: 20 minutes
Cooking Time: 30 minutes

Nutrition Facts

Serving size: 1 bar.

Amount Per Serving	
Calories	235
Calories From Fat (16%)	37.84
	% Daily Value
Total Fat 4.49g	7%
Saturated Fat 0.47g	2%
Cholesterol 0mg	0%
Sodium 160.88mg	7%
Potassium 375.96mg	11%
Total Carbohydrates 47.26g	16%
Fiber 5.12g	20%
Sugar 26.12g	
Protein 5.02g	10%

Date Pecan Cookies

9		medjool dates, pitted and chopped	1/2	cups	almond meal
1/2	cup	sour almond milk	2	tsp	baking powder
1/4	cup	almond milk	1/2	tsp	salt
1	tsp	vanilla	1/3	cup	chopped pecans
1 1/2	cups	whole wheat flour	12		medjool dates, pitted and chopped

Procedure

1 Using a blender, puree 9 chopped dates, sour almond milk, almond milk, and vanilla.

2 Combine flour, almond meal, baking powder, salt, and pecans.

3 Drop 12 chopped dates one by one into the flour mixture and stir to coat the date pieces with flour to prevent them from clumping together.

4 Stir blended date mixture into flour mixture until combined.

5 Drop dough by spoonful onto baking sheet lined with parchment paper.

6 Bake at 350º F for 15 minutes.

Servings: 36
Yield: 36 cookies

Oven Temperature: 350°F

Preparation Time: 30 minutes
Cooking Time: 15 minutes

Nutrition Facts

Serving size: 1 cookie.

Amount Per Serving	
Calories	69.02
Calories From Fat (14%)	9.5
	% Daily Value
Total Fat 1.12g	2%
Saturated Fat 0.09g	<1%
Cholesterol 0mg	0%
Sodium 63.39mg	3%
Potassium 111.34mg	3%
Total Carbohydrates 14.82g	5%
Fiber 1.25g	5%
Sugar 9.39g	
Protein 1.02g	2%

Ginger Molasses Cookies

12		medjool dates, pitted and chopped	2	tsp	baking soda
1/2	cup	sour almond milk	1	tsp	ground cinnamon
1/4	cup	blackstrap molasses	1	tsp	ground ginger
1 1/2	cups	whole wheat flour	1/2	tsp	ground cloves
1/2	cup	almond meal	1/2	tsp	salt

Procedure

1 Using a blender, puree dates, sour almond milk, and molasses.

2 Combine flour, almond meal, baking soda and spices.

3 Stir date mixture into dry ingredients.

4 Drop dough on to baking sheets lined with parchment paper; flatten.

5 Bake at 350° F for 10-12 minutes.

Servings: 36

Oven Temperature: 350°F

Preparation Time: 30 minutes
Cooking Time: 10 minutes

Nutrition Facts

Serving size: 1 cookie.

Amount Per Serving	
Calories	50.34
Calories From Fat (6%)	3.2
	% Daily Value
Total Fat 0.37g	<1%
Saturated Fat 0.03g	<1%
Cholesterol 0mg	0%
Sodium 106.24mg	4%
Potassium 121.52mg	3%
Total Carbohydrates 11.55g	4%
Fiber 0.79g	3%
Sugar 5.35g	
Protein 0.82g	2%

Note

Blackstrap molasses is a sweetener that is actually healthy. It is high in iron and calcium. Molasses is an excellent source of copper and manganese and also a very good source of potassium and magnesium. Look for unsulphured blackstrap molasses because it doesn't contain sulfur, to which some people are sensitive, and it also tastes better.

Source: "Blackstrap molasses" in The World's Healthiest Foods website,
http://www.whfoods.com/genpage.php?dbid=118&tname=foodspice

Oatmeal Spice Cookies

1	cup	raisins	1/2	tsp	baking powder
12		medjool dates, pitted and chopped	1/2	tsp	salt
1	cup	sour almond milk	2	tsp	cinnamon
2	cups	rolled oats	1/4	tsp	nutmeg
1 1/2	cup	whole wheat flour	1/4	tsp	cloves
1/2	cup	almond meal	1/2	cup	chopped walnuts
1	tsp	baking soda			

Procedure

1 Put 1 cup raisins in microwave safe bowl and just cover with water. Heat for 1 minute in microwave.

2 Using a blender, puree dates and sour almond milk.

3 Combine rolled oats, flour, almond meal, baking soda, baking powder, spices and walnuts.

4 Stir date mixture into dry ingredients. Drain raisins and fold into dough.

5 Drop dough on to baking sheet lined with parchment paper.

6 Bake at 350° F for 10-12 minutes.

Servings: 48
Yield: 48 cookies

Oven Temperature: 350°F

Preparation Time: 40 minutes
Cooking Time: 12 minutes

Nutrition Facts

Serving size: 1 cookie.

Amount Per Serving	
Calories	77.84
Calories From Fat (17%)	13.25
	% Daily Value
Total Fat 1.57g	2%
Saturated Fat 0.18g	<1%
Cholesterol 0mg	0%
Sodium 59.98mg	2%
Potassium 109.55mg	3%
Total Carbohydrates 14.89g	5%
Fiber 1.53g	6%
Sugar 6.08g	
Protein 2.02g	4%

Thumbprint Cookies

12		medjool dates, pitted and chopped	1	cup	whole wheat flour
3/4	cup	sour almond milk	1	cup	almond meal
1	tsp	vanilla	1/2	tsp	salt
1	cup	rolled oats	2/3	cup	all fruit jam

Procedure

1 Using a blender, puree dates, sour almond milk, and vanilla.

2 Combine rolled oats, flour, almond meal, and salt.

3 Stir date mixture into dry ingredients.

4 Roll cookie dough into balls and place on baking sheet lined with parchment paper. Make indentation in cookie ball with thumb and fill each cookie with 1 tsp. jam.

5 Bake at 350° F for 15 minutes.

Servings: 30
Yield: 30 cookies

Oven Temperature: 350°F

Preparation Time: 30 minutes
Cooking Time: 15 minutes

Nutrition Facts

Serving size: 1 cookie.

Amount Per Serving	
Calories	80.59
Calories From Fat (12%)	9.5
	% Daily Value
Total Fat 1.1g	2%
Saturated Fat 0.11g	<1%
Cholesterol 0mg	0%
Sodium 43.55mg	2%
Potassium 98.55mg	3%
Total Carbohydrates 16.76g	6%
Fiber 1.45g	6%
Sugar 9.45g	
Protein 1.79g	4%

Apple Crisp

4		large baking apples, peeled, cored and thinly sliced
1/2	cup	date syrup (p. 79)
2	tsp	cinnamon
1/2	tsp	allspice
1/4	tsp	nutmeg

Topping

3/4	cup	rolled oats
1/3	cup	almond meal
1/3	cup	chopped walnuts
1/2	cup	date syrup (p. 79)
1/2	tsp	cinnamon
1/2	tsp	vanilla

Procedure

1 Spray 8" x 11.5" x 2" baking pan with cooking spray.

2 Combine 1/2 cup date syrup, 2 tsp. cinnamon, allspice and nutmeg in a small bowl and mix well.

3 Slice fruit into prepared pan. Spoon in date spice mixture and stir to combine.

4 Bake at 400º F for 30 minutes.

5 To make topping, mix rolled oats, almond meal, walnuts, 1/2 cup date syrup, vanilla and 1/2 tsp. cinnamon together in small bowl.

6 Spread topping over baked apples and bake for an additional 15 minutes.

7 Serve warm.

Servings: 6

Oven Temperature: 400°F

Preparation Time: 40 minutes
Cooking Time: 45 minutes

Nutrition Facts

Serving size: 1/6 of a recipe (5.6 ounces).

Amount Per Serving	
Calories	228.9
Calories From Fat (23%)	51.75
	% Daily Value
Total Fat 6.13g	9%
Saturated Fat 0.65g	3%
Cholesterol 0mg	0%
Sodium 2.2mg	<1%
Potassium 373.27mg	11%
Total Carbohydrates 44.11g	15%
Fiber 5.49g	22%
Sugar 30.41g	
Protein 3.66g	7%

Baked Apples

2	large baking apples		1/2 tsp	cinnamon
4	medjool dates, pitted and chopped		1/4 tsp	nutmeg
1/2 cup	apple juice			

Procedure

1 Core apples. Fill apples with dates and place in baking dish. Combine apple juice and spices; pour over apples.

2 Bake at 350° F for about 1 hour, or until apples are tender, basting occasionally with apple juice.

Servings: 2

Oven Temperature: 350°F

Preparation Time: 15 minutes
Cooking Time: 1 hour

Nutrition Facts

Serving size: 1 apple.

Amount Per Serving	
Calories	236.29
Calories From Fat (2%)	4.15
	% Daily Value
Total Fat 0.5g	<1%
Saturated Fat 0.13g	<1%
Cholesterol 0mg	0%
Sodium 4.45mg	<1%
Potassium 548.12mg	16%
Total Carbohydrates 62.71g	21%
Fiber 7.05g	28%
Sugar 52.3g	
Protein 1.33g	3%

Blueberry Cobbler

Filling

2		packages (12 oz.) frozen blueberries, thawed
1/2	cup	date syrup (p. 79)
1	Tbs	cornstarch

Biscuit Crust

3		dates, pitted and chopped
1/2	cup	sour almond milk
1/2	cup	applesauce
1	cup	whole wheat flour
1 1/2	tsp	baking powder

Procedure

1 Spray 8" square pan with cooking spray.
2 Combine date syrup and cornstarch.
3 Combine blueberries and date syrup/cornstarch mixture in baking pan and microwave for 1-5 minutes, until warm. Stir.
4 Using a blender, puree dates, sour almond milk, and applesauce.
5 Combine flour and baking power.
6 Add date mixture to dry ingredients and stir until just blended.
7 Spoon biscuit crust in mounds on top of the blueberry filling.
8 Bake at 400° F for about 25-30 minutes, until the cobbler crust is golden brown.
9 Serve warm.

Servings: 9

Oven Temperature: 400°F

Preparation Time: 20 minutes
Cooking Time: 30 minutes

Nutrition Facts

Serving size: 1/9 of a recipe (5.1 ounces).

Amount Per Serving	
Calories	152.97
Calories From Fat (5%)	7.18
	% Daily Value
Total Fat 0.86g	1%
Saturated Fat 0.06g	<1%
Cholesterol 0mg	0%
Sodium 93.12mg	4%
Potassium 206.69mg	6%
Total Carbohydrates 36.48g	12%
Fiber 3.88g	16%
Sugar 20.13g	
Protein 2.17g	4%

Cherry Cobbler

Filling

2		packages (12 oz.) frozen cherries, thawed
1/2	cup	date syrup (p. 79)
1	Tbs	cornstarch

Biscuit Crust

3		dates, pitted and chopped
1/2	cup	sour almond milk
1/2	cup	applesauce
1	cup	whole wheat flour
1 1/2	tsp	baking powder

Procedure

1. Spray 8" square pan with cooking spray.
2. Combine date syrup and cornstarch.
3. Combine cherries and date syrup/cornstarch mixture in baking pan and microwave for 1-5 minutes, until warm. Stir.
4. Using a blender, puree dates, almond milk, and applesauce.
5. Combine flour and baking power.
6. Add date mixture to dry ingredients and stir until just blended.
7. Spoon biscuit crust in mounds on top of the cherry filling.
8. Bake at 400° F for about 25-30 minutes, until the cobbler crust is golden brown.
9. Serve warm.

Servings: 9

Oven Temperature: 400°F

Preparation Time: 20 minutes
Cooking Time: 30 minutes

Nutrition Facts

Serving size: 1/9 of a recipe (5.1 ounces).

Amount Per Serving	
Calories	149.09
Calories From Fat (4%)	5.85
	% Daily Value
Total Fat 0.7g	1%
Saturated Fat 0.1g	<1%
Cholesterol 0mg	0%
Sodium 93.11mg	4%
Potassium 259.32mg	7%
Total Carbohydrates 35.58g	12%
Fiber 3.05g	12%
Sugar 20.54g	
Protein 2.55g	5%

Cranberry Pear Crisp

Filling

6		pears, peeled, cored and sliced
1 1/2	cups	cranberries
1/2	cup	date syrup (p. 79)
1	tsp	ground ginger
1/2	tsp	ground cinnamon

Topping

3/4	cup	rolled oats
1/3	cup	almond meal
1/3	cup	chopped walnuts
1/2	cup	date syrup (p. 79)
1/2	tsp	ground cinnamon
1/2	tsp	vanilla

Procedure

1 Spray 8" square pan with cooking spray.

2 Combine 1/2 date syrup, ginger and 1/2 tsp. cinnamon in small bowl and mix well.

3 Slice pears into prepared pan; add cranberries.

4 Spoon in date/spice mixture and stir to combine.

5 To make topping, mix rolled oats, almond meal, walnuts, 1/2 date syrup, vanilla, and 1/2 tsp. cinnamon together. Spread topping over fruit.

6 Bake at 400° F for 30 minutes, until golden brown.

7 Serve warm.

Servings: 9

Oven Temperature: 400°F

Preparation Time: 20 minutes
Cooking Time: 30 minutes

Nutrition Facts

Serving size: 1/9 of a recipe (7.7 ounces).

Amount Per Serving	
Calories	237.71
Calories From Fat (16%)	38.95
	% Daily Value
Total Fat 4.62g	7%
Saturated Fat 0.48g	2%
Cholesterol 0mg	0%
Sodium 2.95mg	<1%
Potassium 407.9mg	12%
Total Carbohydrates 49.54g	17%
Fiber 8.55g	34%
Sugar 28.81g	
Protein 4.17g	8%

Peach Cobbler

Filling

2		packages (12 oz.) frozen peaches, thawed
1/2	cup	date syrup (p. 79)
1	Tbs	cornstarch

Biscuit Crust

3		dates, pitted and chopped
1/2	cup	sour almond milk
1/2	cup	applesauce
1	cup	whole wheat flour
1 1/2	tsp	baking powder

Procedure

1 Spray 8" square pan with cooking spray.

2 Combine date syrup and cornstarch.

3 Combine peaches and date syrup/cornstarch mixture in baking pan and microwave for 1-5 minutes, until warm. Stir.

4 Using a blender, puree dates, sour almond milk, and applesauce.

5 Combine flour and baking power.

6 Add date mixture to dry ingredients and stir until just blended.

7 Spoon biscuit crust in mounds on top of the peach filling.

8 Bake at 400° F for about 25-30 minutes, until the cobbler crust is golden brown.

9 Serve warm.

Servings: 9

Oven Temperature: 400°F

Preparation Time: 20 minutes
Cooking Time: 30 minutes

Nutrition Facts

Serving size: 1/9 of a recipe (5.1 ounces).

Amount Per Serving	
Calories	141.42
Calories From Fat (2%)	3.1
	% Daily Value
Total Fat 0.37g	<1%
Saturated Fat 0.02g	<1%
Cholesterol 0mg	0%
Sodium 92.36mg	4%
Potassium 165.87mg	5%
Total Carbohydrates 34.3g	11%
Fiber 2.92g	12%
Sugar 19.14g	
Protein 2.39g	5%

Peach Crisp

Filling

2		packages (12 oz each) frozen peaches, thawed
1/2	cup	date syrup (p. 79)
1	tsp	cinnamon

Topping

3/4	cup	rolled oats
1/3	cup	almond meal
1/3	cup	chopped walnuts
1/2	cup	date syrup (p. 79)
1/2	tsp	ground cinnamon
1/2	tsp	vanilla

Procedure

1 Spray 8" square pan with cooking spray.

2 Combine 1/2 cup date syrup and 1 tsp. cinnamon in a small bowl and mix well.

3 Pour fruit into prepared pan. Spoon in date mixture and stir to combine.

4 To make topping, combine rolled oats, almond meal, walnuts, 1/2 cup date syrup, 1/2 tsp. cinnamon and vanilla together in small bowl. Spread topping over peaches.

5 Bake at 350º F for 30 minutes, until the topping is golden brown.

6 Serve warm.

Servings: 6

Oven Temperature: 350°F

Preparation Time: 15 minutes
Cooking Time: 30 minutes

Nutrition Facts

Serving size: 1/6 of a recipe (7.3 ounces).

Amount Per Serving	
Calories	263.46
Calories From Fat (21%)	56.03
	% Daily Value
Total Fat 6.64g	10%
Saturated Fat 0.7g	4%
Cholesterol 0mg	0%
Sodium 1.77mg	<1%
Potassium 339.31mg	10%
Total Carbohydrates 49.3g	16%
Fiber 6.81g	27%
Sugar 29.72g	
Protein 6.17g	12%

Persian Fruit Salad

2	oranges, peeled and chopped	6	dates, pitted and chopped
1	small red grapefruit, peeled and chopped	1	medium apples, peeled, cored, and chopped
1/2 cup	chopped dried figs		
		1/8 cup	dry-toasted sliced almonds

Procedure

Combine oranges, grapefruit, figs, dates and apple into medium bowl. When chopping oranges and grapefruit, squeeze the juice from their peels into fruit salad.

Servings: 6

Preparation Time: 15 minutes

Nutrition Facts

Serving size: 1/6 of a recipe (5.3 ounces).

Amount Per Serving	
Calories	166.55
Calories From Fat (9%)	15.18
	% Daily Value
Total Fat 1.81g	3%
Saturated Fat 0.16g	<1%
Cholesterol 0mg	0%
Sodium 2.26mg	<1%
Potassium 429.37mg	12%
Total Carbohydrates 39.93g	13%
Fiber 5.37g	21%
Sugar 31.23g	
Protein 2.25g	5%

Warm Fruit Salad

1	cup	frozen strawberries	1/2	cup	frozen peaches, chopped
1	cup	frozen blueberries	6		medjool dates, pitted chopped
1/2	cup	frozen mangoes, chopped	1		apple, peeled, cored, and chopped

Procedure

1 Combine all ingredients in saucepan and simmer for 40-50 minutes, until apple is soft and frozen fruit is heated.

2 Serve warm.

Servings: 6

Preparation Time: 15 minutes
Cooking Time: 50 minutes

Nutrition Facts

Serving size: 1/6 of a recipe (4.9 ounces).

Amount Per Serving	
Calories	123.37
Calories From Fat (2%)	2.27
	% Daily Value
Total Fat 0.27g	<1%
Saturated Fat 0.02g	<1%
Cholesterol 0mg	0%
Sodium 1.24mg	<1%
Potassium 254.7mg	7%
Total Carbohydrates 32.67g	11%
Fiber 4.08g	16%
Sugar 26.59g	
Protein 1.04g	2%

Apple Pie

Crust

1	cup	walnuts
6		medjool dates, pitted and chopped

Filling

5		apples, cored, seeded, skinned and thinly sliced
1/2	cup	date syrup (p. 79)

1	tsp	cinnamon
1/2	tsp	nutmeg

Crumble Topping

1	cup	rolled oats
1/2	cup	date syrup (p. 79)
1	tsp	cinnamon

Procedure

To Make the Crust

1 Grind walnuts in food processor until fine.

2 Add chopped dates and process until mixture adheres together.

3 Spray 9" pie pan with cooking spray.

4 Press walnut date mixture evenly into pie pan.

To Make the Filling

1 Combine 1/2 cup date syrup, 1 tsp. cinnamon, and nutmeg in small bowl and mix well.

2 Gently stir date syrup/spice mixture into apple slices in large bowl.

3 Arrange apple slice in walnut crust.

To Make the Topping

1 Combine rolled oats, 1/2 cup date syrup, and 1 tsp. cinnamon in a small bowl and crumble over apples.

Baking the Pie

1 Cover crust with pie shield to prevent crust from burning.

2 Bake pie at 350° F and bake for 30 minutes.

3 Remove pie from oven and crumble topping over pie.

4 Return pie to oven and bake for another 30 minutes.

Servings: 8

Oven Temperature: 350°F

Preparation Time: 40 minutes
Cooking Time: 1 hour

Nutrition Facts

Serving size: 1 slice.

Amount Per Serving	
Calories	336.04
Calories From Fat (28%)	92.96
	% Daily Value
Total Fat 11.11g	17%
Saturated Fat 1.2g	6%
Cholesterol 0mg	0%
Sodium 2.7mg	<1%
Potassium 536.75mg	15%
Total Carbohydrates 58.93g	20%
Fiber 8.2g	33%
Sugar 37.36g	
Protein 6.54g	13%

Banana Pie

Crust

1	cup	almond meal
6		medjool dates, pitted and chopped

Vanilla Pudding

3	cups	almond milk

12		medjool dates, pitted and chopped
1	tsp	vanilla
1/4	cup	cornstarch
2		bananas

Procedure

To Make the Crust

1 Combine almond meal and 6 chopped dates in food processor and process until mixture adheres together.

2 Spray 9" pie pan with cooking spray.

3 Press almond date mixture evenly into pie pan.

4 Bake at 350° F for 10 minutes.

To Make the Pudding

1 Using a blender, puree 12 chopped dates, almond milk, vanilla and cornstarch.

2 Pour into top of double boiler and cook for about 10 minutes, stirring constantly, until the pudding is thick.

3 Pour pudding into a bowl and cover surface with plastic wrap so a crust doesn't form on the top as the pudding cools.

To Make the Pie

1 When pudding and crust have cooled, slice bananas and layer slices on bottom and sides of pie crust.

2 Pour pudding into crust on top of bananas.

3 Refrigerate for several hours before serving.

Servings: 8

Oven Temperature: 350°F

Preparation Time: 30 minutes
Cooking Time: 20 minutes

Nutrition Facts

Serving size: 1 slice.

Amount Per Serving	
Calories	234.59
Calories From Fat (14%)	32.3
	% Daily Value
Total Fat 3.74g	6%
Saturated Fat 0.18g	<1%
Cholesterol 0mg	0%
Sodium 68.74mg	3%
Potassium 553.6mg	16%
Total Carbohydrates 52.44g	17%
Fiber 5.25g	21%
Sugar 39.72g	
Protein 2.73g	5%

Variation

Use Carob Pie Crust (p. 46) in place of Almond Pie Crust.

Blueberry Pie

Crust

1	cup	almond meal
6		dates, pitted and chopped

Filling

24	oz	fresh blueberries, divided
1/2	cup	date syrup (p. 79)
1	Tbs	cornstarch

Procedure

To Make the Crust

1 Combine almond meal and dates in food processor and process until mixture adheres together.

2 Spray 9" pie pan with cooking spray.

3 Press almond date mixture evenly into pie pan.

4 Bake at 350° F for 10 minutes. Cool.

To Make the Filling

1 Set 2 cups of blueberries aside. Put remainder of blueberries into saucepan.

2 Mix date syrup and cornstarch together until well blended.

3 Add date cornstarch mixture to blueberries in pan.

4 Bring to a boil, stirring frequently. Reduce heat and simmer until blueberries release their juices and the mixture is thick, about 10 minutes.

5 Remove from heat and cool for about 5 minutes.

To Make the Pie

1 Stir in reserved blueberries into cooled cooked blueberries and mix gently.

2 Pour blueberries into prepared pie shell.

3 Refrigerate at least two hours before serving.

Servings: 8

Oven Temperature: 350°F

Preparation Time: 40 minutes
Cooking Time: 20 minutes

Nutrition Facts

Serving size: 1 slice.

Amount Per Serving	
Calories	162.89
Calories From Fat (14%)	22.63
	% Daily Value
Total Fat 2.58g	4%
Saturated Fat 0.17g	<1%
Cholesterol 0mg	0%
Sodium 1.55mg	<1%
Potassium 274.68mg	8%
Total Carbohydrates 36.5g	12%
Fiber 4.51g	18%
Sugar 28.58g	
Protein 2.23g	4%

Carob Pie

Carob Crust

3/4	cup	almond meal
1/4	cup	carob powder
6		medjool dates, pitted and chopped
1	tsp	vanilla

Carob Pudding

12		medjool dates, pitted and chopped
3	cups	almond milk
1	tsp	vanilla
1/3	cup	carob powder
1/4	cup	cornstarch

Procedure

To Make the Crust

1 Combine almond meal, 1/4 cup carob powder, 6 chopped dates, and 1 tsp. vanilla in a food processor until mixture adheres together.

2 Spray 9" pie pan with cooking spray.

3 Press almond carob mixture into pie pan.

4 Bake at 350º F for 10 minutes. Cool.

To Make the Pudding

1 Using a blender, puree 12 chopped dates, almond milk, 1 tsp. vanilla, 1/3 cup carob powder and cornstarch.

2 Pour into top of double boiler and cook for about 10 minutes, stirring constantly, until the pudding is thick.

3 Pour pudding into a bowl and cover surface with plastic wrap so a crust doesn't form on the top as the pudding cools.

To Make the Pie

1 When pudding and crust have cooled, pour pudding into crust.

2 Refrigerate for several hours before serving.

Servings: 8

Oven Temperature: 350°F

Preparation Time: 20 minutes
Cooking Time: 20 minutes

Nutrition Facts

Serving size: 1 slice.

Amount Per Serving	
Calories	226.42
Calories From Fat (12%)	26.5
	% Daily Value
Total Fat 3.08g	5%
Saturated Fat 0.11g	<1%
Cholesterol 0mg	0%
Sodium 68.49mg	3%
Potassium 448.76mg	13%
Total Carbohydrates 51.41g	17%
Fiber 6.7g	27%
Sugar 38.47g	
Protein 2.15g	4%

Date Pie

This pie has a rich caramel flavor.

Crust

1	cup	almond meal
6		medjool dates, pitted and chopped

Date Pudding

24		medjool dates, pitted and chopped
3	cups	almond milk
1	tsp	vanilla
1/4	cup	cornstarch

Procedure

To Make the Crust

1 Combine almond meal and 6 chopped dates in a food processor until mixture adheres together.

2 Spray 9" pie pan with cooking spray.

3 Press almond date mixture into pie pan.

4 Bake at 350° F for 10 minutes. Cool.

To Make the Pudding

1 Using a blender, puree 24 chopped dates, almond milk, vanilla and cornstarch.

2 Pour into top of double boiler and cook for about 10 minutes, stirring constantly, until the pudding is thick.

3 Pour pudding into a bowl and cover surface with plastic wrap so a crust doesn't form on the top as the pudding cools.

To Make the Pie

1 When pudding and crust have cooled, pour pudding into crust.

2 Refrigerate for several hours before serving.

Servings: 8

Oven Temperature: 350°F

Preparation Time: 20 minutes
Cooking Time: 20 minutes

Nutrition Facts

Serving size: 1 slice.

Amount Per Serving	
Calories	308.05
Calories From Fat (10%)	31.93
	% Daily Value
Total Fat 3.7g	6%
Saturated Fat 0.15g	<1%
Cholesterol 0mg	0%
Sodium 68.81mg	3%
Potassium 698.55mg	20%
Total Carbohydrates 72.69g	24%
Fiber 6.89g	28%
Sugar 60.04g	
Protein 3.06g	6%

Peach Pie

Crust

| 1 | cup | almond meal |
| 6 | | medjool dates, pitted and chopped |

Peach Filling

2	lbs	fresh peaches, peeled and thinly sliced, divided
1/2	cup	date syrup (p. 79)
1	Tbs	cornstarch

Procedure

To Make the Crust

1 Combine almond meal and 6 chopped dates in food processor and process until mixture adheres together.
2 Spray 9" pie pan with cooking spray.
3 Press almond date mixture evenly into pie pan.
4 Bake at 350° F for 10 minutes. Cool.

To Make the Filling

1 Chop 2 cups peaches and put in medium saucepan.
2 Mix date syrup and cornstarch together until well blended.
3 Add date mixture to peaches in saucepan.
4 Simmer peaches until soft, about 5-10 minutes, stirring often. Mash peaches with a potato masher.
5 Remove from heat and cool for about 5 minutes.

To Make the Pie

1 Stir reserved peaches into cooked peaches and mix gently.
2 Pour peaches into prepared pie shell.
3 Refrigerate at least two hours before serving.

Servings: 8

Oven Temperature: 350°F

Preparation Time: 20 minutes
Cooking Time: 20 minutes

Nutrition Facts

Serving size: 1 slice.

Amount Per Serving	
Calories	158.65
Calories From Fat (14%)	22.49
	% Daily Value
Total Fat 2.56g	4%
Saturated Fat 0.17g	<1%
Cholesterol 0mg	0%
Sodium 0.71mg	<1%
Potassium 424.65mg	12%
Total Carbohydrates 34.98g	12%
Fiber 4.12g	16%
Sugar 29.63g	
Protein 2.63g	5%

Recipe Tips

Use 2 packages (12 oz) frozen peaches, thawed and drained, in place of fresh peaches.

Pecan Pie

Carob Cookie Crust

3/4	cup	almond meal
1/4	cup	carob powder
6		dates, pitted and chopped
1	tsp	vanilla

Filling

24		medjool dates, pitted and chopped
2	cups	almond milk
1	tsp	vanilla
1/4	cup	cornstarch
1	cup	pecan halves

Procedure

To Make the Crust

1 Combine almond meal, carob powder, 6 chopped dates and vanilla in food processor until mixture adheres together.
2 Spray 9" pie pan with cooking spray.
3 Press almond carob mixture evenly into pie pan.

To Make the Filling

1 Using a blender, puree 24 chopped dates, almond milk, vanilla and cornstarch.

To Make the Pie

1 Place pecans on bottom and sides of pie crust.
2 Pour filling into crust on top of pecans.
3 Cover crust with pie shield to prevent crust from burning.
4 Bake at 325° F for 45 minutes.

Servings: 8

Oven Temperature: 325°F

Preparation Time: 25 minutes
Cooking Time: 45 minutes

Nutrition Facts

Serving size: 1 slice.

Amount Per Serving	
Calories	399.47
Calories From Fat (26%)	103.64
	% Daily Value
Total Fat 12.29g	19%
Saturated Fat 0.95g	5%
Cholesterol 0mg	0%
Sodium 35.1mg	1%
Potassium 719.56mg	21%
Total Carbohydrates 76.58g	26%
Fiber 8.9g	36%
Sugar 61.61g	
Protein 3.86g	8%

Variation

Make almond crust instead of carob crust by omitting carob powder and vanilla and using 1 cup almond meal.

Pumpkin Pie

Crust

1	cup	pecans
6		medjool dates, pitted and chopped

Custard Filling

6		medjool dates, pitted and chopped
1 1/2	cups	almond milk

15	oz	can pumpkin
1/2	tsp	salt
1	tsp	cinnamon
1/2	tsp	ground ginger
1/4	tsp	ground cloves
1/4	cup	cornstarch

Procedure

To Make the Crust

1 Grind pecans in food processor until fine.

2 Add 6 chopped dates and process until mixture adheres together.

3 Spray 9" pie pan with cooking spray.

4 Press pecan date mixture evenly into pie pan.

To Make the Filling

1 Using a blender, puree 6 chopped dates, almond milk, pumpkin, spices and cornstarch.

To Make the Pie

1 Pour custard filling into pecan nut crust.

2 Cover crust with a pie crust shield to prevent crust from burning.

3 Bake at 350° F for 45-50 minutes or until firm.

4 Refrigerate before serving. Serve with Nut Cream (p.16) topping, if desired.

Servings: 8

Oven Temperature: 350°F

Preparation Time: 30 minutes
Cooking Time: 50 minutes

Nutrition Facts

Serving size: 1 slice.

Amount Per Serving	
Calories	235.8
Calories From Fat (38%)	89.42
	% Daily Value
Total Fat 10.69g	16%
Saturated Fat 0.92g	5%
Cholesterol 0mg	0%
Sodium 182.68mg	8%
Potassium 454.34mg	13%
Total Carbohydrates 37.53g	13%
Fiber 5.68g	23%
Sugar 26.24g	
Protein 2.7g	5%

Strawberry Pie

Crust

1	cup	almond meal
6		dates, pitted and chopped

Filling

2	lbs	fresh strawberries, divided
1/2	cup	date syrup (p. 79)
1	Tbsp	cornstarch

Procedure

To Make the Crust

1 Combine almond meal and dates in a food processor and process until mixture adheres together.

2 Spray a 9" pie pan with cooking spray.

3 Press almond date mixture evenly into pie pan.

4 Bake at 350° F for 10 minutes. Cool.

To Make the Filling

1 Chop 3/4 pounds strawberries and put in medium saucepan.

2 Mix date syrup and cornstarch together until well blended.

3 Add date mixture to strawberries in pan. Simmer strawberries until soft, about 5-10 minutes.

4 Mash strawberries with a potato masher.

5 Remove from heat and cool for about 5 minutes.

To Make the Pie

1 Stir reserved strawberries into cooked strawberries and mix gently.

2 Pour strawberries into prepared pie shell.

3 Refrigerate at least two hours before serving.

Servings: 8

Oven Temperature: 350°F

Preparation Time: 40 minutes
Cooking Time: 20 minutes

Nutrition Facts

Serving size: 1 slice.

Amount Per Serving	
Calories	150.7
Calories From Fat (15%)	23.11
	% Daily Value
Total Fat 2.64g	4%
Saturated Fat 0.17g	<1%
Cholesterol 0mg	0%
Sodium 1.84mg	<1%
Potassium 382.69mg	11%
Total Carbohydrates 32.89g	11%
Fiber 4.74g	19%
Sugar 25.66g	
Protein 2.36g	5%

Variation

Make Carob Pie Crust (p.46) instead of Almond Pie Crust.

Sweet Potato Pie

Pecan Crust

1	cup	pecans
6		medjool dates, pitted and chopped

Custard Filling

1 1/2	lbs	sweet potatoes (about 2 medium)
6		medjool dates, pitted and chopped

1 1/2	cups	almond milk
1/2	tsp	salt
1	tsp	cinnamon
1/2	tsp	nutmeg
1/4	cup	cornstarch

Procedure

To Make the Filling

1 Bake sweet potatoes at 450° F for 45-50 minutes, until very soft. Cool.

2 Peel sweet potatoes and mash with a fork. Measure out 2 cups of mashed sweet potatoes.

3 Using a blender, puree 6 chopped dates, almond milk, 2 cups mashed sweet potatoes, spices and cornstarch.

To Make the Crust

1 Grind pecans in food processor until fine.

2 Add 6 chopped dates and process until mixture adheres together.

3 Spray 9" pie pan with cooking spray.

4 Press pecan date mixture into pie pan.

To Make the Pie

1 Pour custard into pecan nut crust.

2 Cover crust with a pie crust shield to prevent crust from getting burned.

3 Bake at 350° F for 45-50 minutes or until firm.

4 Refrigerate before serving. Serve with Nut Cream (p.16) topping, if desired.

Servings: 8

Oven Temperature: 350°F

Preparation Time: 30 minutes
Cooking Time: 1 1/2 hours

Nutrition Facts

Serving size: 1 slice.

Amount Per Serving	
Calories	275.97
Calories From Fat (33%)	90.6
	% Daily Value
Total Fat 10.81g	17%
Saturated Fat 0.92g	5%
Cholesterol 0.85mg	<1%
Sodium 191.77mg	8%
Potassium 475.06mg	14%
Total Carbohydrates 46.19g	15%
Fiber 5.68g	23%
Sugar 27.92g	
Protein 3.19g	6%

Carob Pudding

12	medjool dates, pitted and chopped		1/3 cup	carob powder
3	cups almond milk		3 Tbs	cornstarch
1	tsp vanilla			

Procedure

1 Using a blender, puree dates, almond milk, vanilla, carob powder and cornstarch.

2 Pour into top of double boiler and cook for about 10 minutes, stirring constantly, until the pudding is thick.

3 Pour pudding into a bowl and cover surface with plastic wrap so a crust doesn't form on the top as the pudding cools.

4 Refrigerate for several hours before serving.

Servings: 7
Yield: 3 1/2 cups

Preparation Time: 15 minutes
Cooking Time: 10 minutes

Nutrition Facts

Serving size: 1/2 cup.

Amount Per Serving	
Calories	156.79
Calories From Fat (8%)	12.94
	% Daily Value
Total Fat 1.56g	2%
Saturated Fat 0g	0%
Cholesterol 0mg	0%
Sodium 77.81mg	3%
Potassium 368.74mg	11%
Total Carbohydrates 37.67g	13%
Fiber 4.73g	19%
Sugar 28.95g	
Protein 1.18g	2%

Date Pudding

This pudding has a rich caramel flavor.

| 24 | | medjool dates, pitted and chopped | 1 | tsp | vanilla |
| 3 | cups | almond milk | 3 | Tbs | cornstarch |

Procedure

1 Using a blender, puree dates, almond milk, vanilla and cornstarch.

2 Pour into top of double boiler and cook for about 10 minutes, stirring constantly, until the pudding is thick.

3 Pour pudding into a bowl and cover surface with plastic wrap so a crust doesn't form on the top as the pudding cools.

4 When pudding has cooled, refrigerate for several hours before serving.

Servings: 8
Yield: 4 cups

Preparation Time: 10 minutes
Cooking Time: 10 minutes

Nutrition Facts

Serving size: 1/2 cup.

Amount Per Serving	
Calories	398.83
Calories From Fat (3%)	11.97
	% Daily Value
Total Fat 1.44g	2%
Saturated Fat 0g	0%
Cholesterol 0mg	0%
Sodium 72.59mg	3%
Potassium 574.59mg	16%
Total Carbohydrates 98.6g	33%
Fiber 5.63g	23%
Sugar 47.92g	
Protein 1.8g	4%

Vanilla Pudding

12		medjool dates, pitted and chopped	1	tsp	vanilla
3	cups	almond milk	3	Tbs	cornstarch

Procedure

1 Using a blender, puree dates, almond milk, vanilla and cornstarch.

2 Pour into top of double boiler and cook for about 10 minutes, stirring constantly, until the pudding is thick.

3 Pour pudding into a bowl and cover surface with plastic wrap so a crust doesn't form on the top as the pudding cools.

4 Refrigerate for several hours before serving.

Servings: 7
Yield: 3 1/2 cups

Preparation Time: 15 minutes
Cooking Time: 10 minutes

Nutrition Facts

Serving size: 1/2 cup.

Amount Per Serving	
Calories	141.55
Calories From Fat (9%)	12.94
	% Daily Value
Total Fat 1.56g	2%
Saturated Fat 0g	0%
Cholesterol 0mg	0%
Sodium 77.81mg	3%
Potassium 368.74mg	11%
Total Carbohydrates 33.86g	11%
Fiber 3.21g	13%
Sugar 27.42g	
Protein 1.18g	2%

Apple Walnut Bread

12		medjool dates, pitted and chopped	1	tsp	cinnamon
3/4	cup	sour almond milk	1/2	tsp	nutmeg
1	cup	applesauce	1/2	tsp	salt
1 1/2	cups	whole wheat flour	1/3	cup	chopped walnuts
1/2	cup	almond meal	2		apples, peeled, cored and shredded
1	tsp	baking soda			

Procedure

1 Using a blender, puree dates, sour almond milk, and applesauce.

2 Combine flour, almond meal, baking soda, spices, salt and walnuts.

3 Stir date mixture into dry ingredients until just blended.

4 Fold in apples.

5 Spray 9" loaf pan with cooking spray. Spoon batter into pan.

6 Bake at 350 F for 50-55 minutes.

Servings: 10

Oven Temperature: 350°F

Preparation Time: 15 minutes
Cooking Time: 55 minutes

Nutrition Facts

Serving size: 1 slice.

Amount Per Serving	
Calories	213.15
Calories From Fat (16%)	34.27
	% Daily Value
Total Fat 4.05g	6%
Saturated Fat 0.37g	2%
Cholesterol 0mg	0%
Sodium 257.18mg	11%
Potassium 301.08mg	9%
Total Carbohydrates 43.71g	15%
Fiber 4.04g	16%
Sugar 24.55g	
Protein 3.68g	7%

Banana Bread

12		medjool dates, pitted and chopped	1/2	cup	almond meal
1/4	cup	sour almond milk	1	tsp	baking soda
1/2	cup	applesauce	1/2	tsp	salt
3		ripe bananas, mashed	1/3	cup	chopped walnuts
1 1/2	cups	whole wheat flour			

Procedure

1 Combine flour, almond meal, baking soda, salt and walnuts together.
2 Using a blender, puree dates, sour almond milk, and applesauce. Add bananas and blend lightly.
3 Add the date/banana mixture to the flour mixture and stir until combined.
4 Spray 9" loaf pan with cooking spray. Spoon batter into pan.
5 Bake at 350° F for 50-55 minutes.

Servings: 10

Oven Temperature: 350°F

Preparation Time: 15 minutes
Cooking Time: 55 minutes

Nutrition Facts

Serving size: 1 slice.

Amount Per Serving	
Calories	221.96
Calories From Fat (15%)	32.94
	% Daily Value
Total Fat 3.89g	6%
Saturated Fat 0.37g	2%
Cholesterol 0mg	0%
Sodium 247.97mg	10%
Potassium 378.24mg	11%
Total Carbohydrates 46.24g	15%
Fiber 3.96g	16%
Sugar 24.83g	
Protein 3.9g	8%

Recipe Tips

Turn any quick bread recipe into muffins by spooning batter into muffin pan and baking at 400° F for 25 minutes.

Blueberry Muffins

12		medjool dates, pitted and chopped	1/2	cup	almond meal
1	cup	sour almond milk	1	tsp	baking soda
1/2	cup	almond milk	1/2	tsp	salt
1/2	cup	applesauce	2	cups	fresh or frozen blueberries
1 1/2	cups	whole wheat flour			

Procedure

1 Using a blender, puree dates, sour almond milk, almond milk, and applesauce.

2 Combine flour, almond meal, baking soda and salt.

3 Stir date mixture into dry ingredients. Gently fold in blueberries.

4 Spray muffin pan with cooking spray. Spoon batter into muffin pan.

5 Bake at 400° F for 25 minutes.

Servings: 12

Oven Temperature: 400°F

Preparation Time: 15 minutes
Cooking Time: 25 minutes

Nutrition Facts

Serving size: 1 muffin.

Amount Per Serving	
Calories	154.8
Calories From Fat (9%)	13.32
	% Daily Value
Total Fat 1.55g	2%
Saturated Fat 0.09g	<1%
Cholesterol 0mg	0%
Sodium 225.29mg	9%
Potassium 229mg	7%
Total Carbohydrates 34.71g	12%
Fiber 3.11g	12%
Sugar 19.18g	
Protein 2.65g	5%

Cornbread

12		medjool dates, pitted and chopped	1	cup	whole wheat flour
1/2	cup	sour almond milk	1	cup	cornmeal
3/4	cup	almond milk	1	Tbs	baking powder
1/2	cup	applesauce	1/2	tsp	salt

Procedure

1 Using a blender, puree dates, almond milk, and applesauce.

2 Combine flour, cornmeal, baking powder and salt.

3 Stir the date mixture into the dry ingredients until just blended.

4 Spray 8" square pan with cooking spray. Spoon batter into pan.

5 Bake at 350° F for 20 minutes.

Servings: 9

Oven Temperature: 350°F

Preparation Time: 15 minutes
Cooking Time: 20 minutes

Nutrition Facts

Serving size: 1 slice.

Amount Per Serving	
Calories	200.33
Calories From Fat (5%)	9.75
	% Daily Value
Total Fat 1.17g	2%
Saturated Fat 0.09g	<1%
Cholesterol 0mg	0%
Sodium 322.34mg	13%
Potassium 313.24mg	9%
Total Carbohydrates 47.24g	16%
Fiber 3.8g	15%
Sugar 22.67g	
Protein 3.28g	7%

Date Pecan Bread

12		medjool dates, pitted and chopped	1/2	cup	almond meal
1	cup	sour almond milk	1	tsp	baking soda
1	cup	applesauce	1/2	tsp	salt
1	tsp	vanilla	1/3	cup	chopped pecans
1 1/2	cups	whole wheat flour	9		medjool dates, pitted and chopped

Procedure

1 Using a blender, puree 12 chopped dates, sour almond milk, applesauce and vanilla.

2 Combine flour, almond meal, baking soda, salt and pecans.

3 Drop 9 chopped dates one by one into the flour mixture and stir to coat the date pieces with flour to prevent them from clumping together.

4 Stir the date mixture into the dry ingredients until just blended.

5 Spray 9" loaf pan with cooking spray. Spoon batter into pan.

6 Bake at 350° F for 55 minutes.

Servings: 10

Oven Temperature: 350°F

Preparation Time: 20 minutes
Cooking Time: 55 minutes

Nutrition Facts

Serving size: 1 slice.

Amount Per Serving	
Calories	259.2
Calories From Fat (14%)	35.12
	% Daily Value
Total Fat 4.15g	6%
Saturated Fat 0.32g	2%
Cholesterol 0mg	0%
Sodium 261.53mg	11%
Potassium 423.43mg	12%
Total Carbohydrates 55.9g	19%
Fiber 4.78g	19%
Sugar 36.1g	
Protein 3.74g	7%

Gingerbread

12		medjool dates, pitted and chopped	1	cup	almond meal
1	cup	sour almond milk	1	tsp	baking soda
1/2	cup	almond milk	1	tsp	ground ginger
1/2	cup	applesauce	1	tsp	ground cinnamon
1/4	cup	blackstrap molasses	1/2	tsp	salt
1 1/3	cups	whole wheat flour			

Procedure

1 Using a blender, puree dates, sour almond milk, almond milk, applesauce, and molasses.

2 Combine flour, almond meal, baking soda, and spices.

3 Stir the date mixture into the dry ingredients until just blended.

4 Pour into 8" x 11.5" x 2" baking pan.

5 Bake at 350° F for 30 minutes.

6 Serve with Nut Cream (p.16), if desired.

Servings: 12

Oven Temperature: 350°F

Preparation Time: 15 minutes
Cooking Time: 30 minutes

Nutrition Facts

Serving size: 1 piece.

Amount Per Serving	
Calories	161.03
Calories From Fat (11%)	18.46
	% Daily Value
Total Fat 2.12g	3%
Saturated Fat 0.12g	<1%
Cholesterol 0mg	0%
Sodium 228.8mg	10%
Potassium 385.11mg	11%
Total Carbohydrates 34.85g	12%
Fiber 2.64g	11%
Sugar 17.05g	
Protein 2.72g	5%

Orange Cranberry Bread

12		medjool dates, pitted and chopped	1	tsp	baking soda
3/4	cup	orange juice	1/2	tsp	salt
1	cup	applesauce	1	Tbs	grated orange zest
1	tsp	vanilla extract	1/3	cup	chopped pecans
1 1/2	cup	whole wheat flour	1 1/2	cups	chopped fresh or frozen, unthawed cranberries
1/2	cup	almond meal			

Procedure

1 Using a blender, puree dates, orange juice, applesauce and vanilla.

2 Combine flour, almond meal, baking soda, salt, orange zest, and pecans.

3 Stir the date mixture into the dry ingredients until just blended.

4 Fold in cranberries.

5 Spray 9" loaf pan with cooking spray. Spoon batter into pan.

6 Bake at 350° F for 55 minutes.

Servings: 10

Oven Temperature: 350°F

Preparation Time: 15 minutes
Cooking Time: 55 minutes

Nutrition Facts

Serving size: 1 slice.

Amount Per Serving	
Calories	211.93
Calories From Fat (15%)	32.47
	% Daily Value
Total Fat 3.83g	6%
Saturated Fat 0.32g	2%
Cholesterol 0mg	0%
Sodium 243.85mg	10%
Potassium 306.61mg	9%
Total Carbohydrates 43.6g	15%
Fiber 4.09g	16%
Sugar 23.97g	
Protein 3.46g	7%

Pecan Biscuit Twists

Dough

1 1/2	cups	whole wheat flour
1/2	cup	almond meal
1	Tbs	baking powder
1/2	tsp	salt
1/2	cup	sour almond milk
1/2	cup	almond milk

1/2	cup	applesauce

Topping

2/3	cup	date syrup (p. 79)
1/3	cup	pecans, finely chopped
1	tsp	cinnamon

Procedure

1 Combine flour, almond meal, baking powder and salt.

2 Mix sour almond milk, almond milk and applesauce together and stir into dry ingredients until dough clings together.

3 Knead gently dough in bowl for 12-15 strokes.

4 Roll dough between pieces of plastic wrap into 15 x 8 inch rectangle.

5 Combine date syrup, pecans and cinnamon. Spread topping over dough.

6 Fold dough in half lengthwise to make 15 x 4 inch rectangle. Cut into 1 inch wide strips.

7 Holding strips at both ends, carefully twist in opposite directions twice. Place biscuits on baking sheet lined with parchment paper, pressing both ends down onto baking sheet

8 Bake at 400º F for 10 minutes.

Servings: 12

Oven Temperature: 400°F

Preparation Time: 45 minutes
Cooking Time: 10 minutes

Nutrition Facts

Serving size: 1 piece.

Amount Per Serving	
Calories	118.04
Calories From Fat (24%)	28.79
	% Daily Value
Total Fat 3.4g	5%
Saturated Fat 0.26g	1%
Cholesterol 0mg	0%
Sodium 234.62mg	10%
Potassium 109.59mg	3%
Total Carbohydrates 20.41g	7%
Fiber 1.71g	7%
Sugar 6.5g	
Protein 2.5g	5%

Pumpkin Bread

12		medjool dates, pitted and chopped	1	tsp	cinnamon
1/2	cup	sour almond milk	1/2	tsp	salt
1	can (15 oz)	pumpkin	1/2	tsp	ground ginger
1 1/2	cups	whole wheat flour	1/4	tsp	ground cloves
1/2	cup	almond meal	1/3	cup	chopped pecans
1	tsp	baking soda			

Procedure

1 Using a blender, puree dates and sour almond milk.

2 Add pumpkin to blender and puree. Mixture will be very thick.

3 Combine flour, almond meal, baking soda, spices and pecans.

4 Stir the date mixture into the dry ingredients until just blended.

5 Spray 9" loaf pan with cooking spray. Spoon batter into pan.

6 Bake at 350° F for 50-55 minutes.

Servings: 10

Oven Temperature: 350°F

Preparation Time: 15 minutes
Cooking Time: 55 minutes

Nutrition Facts

Serving size: 1 slice.

Amount Per Serving	
Calories	200.28
Calories From Fat (17%)	33.61
	% Daily Value
Total Fat 3.96g	6%
Saturated Fat 0.38g	2%
Cholesterol 0mg	0%
Sodium 249.59mg	10%
Potassium 329.9mg	9%
Total Carbohydrates 40.45g	13%
Fiber 4.38g	18%
Sugar 20.81g	
Protein 3.72g	7%

Scones

1 1/2	cups	whole wheat flour	1/4	tsp	salt
1	cup	almond meal	1	cup	sour almond milk
4	tsp	baking powder	1/4	cup	date syrup (p. 79)

Procedure

1 Combine flour, almond meal, baking powder and salt.

2 Combine sour almond milk and date syrup.

3 Stir date mixture into dry ingredients until just combined.

4 Fold in fruit or nuts, if using.

5 Using your hands, form dough into 12 scones and place on a baking sheet lined with parchment paper.

6 Bake at 400° F for 12 minutes.

Servings: 12

Oven Temperature: 400°F

Preparation Time: 15 minutes
Cooking Time: 12 minutes

Nutrition Facts

Serving size: 1 scone.

Amount Per Serving	
Calories	90.27
Calories From Fat (19%)	16.97
	% Daily Value
Total Fat 1.94g	3%
Saturated Fat 0.12g	<1%
Cholesterol 0mg	0%
Sodium 226.44mg	9%
Potassium 60.83mg	2%
Total Carbohydrates 16.01g	5%
Fiber 1.06g	4%
Sugar 2.81g	
Protein 2.47g	5%

Variations

Add 1/2 cups chopped nuts or dried fruit such as diced apricots, cranberries, currants, chopped dates, raisins, etc.; add 1 cup fresh or frozen fruit such as blueberries, cranberries, diced peaches, etc.

Zucchini Bread

12		medjool dates, pitted and chopped	1	tsp	baking soda
1	cup	sour almond milk	1	tsp	cinnamon
1	tsp	vanilla	1/2	tsp	salt
1 1/2	cups	whole wheat flour	1/3	cup	chopped walnuts
1/2	cup	almond meal	2		medium zucchini, shredded

Procedure

1 Using a blender, puree dates, sour almond milk and vanilla.

2 Combine flour, almond meal, baking soda, spices and walnuts.

3 Stir date mixture into dry ingredients until just blended.

4 Fold in zucchini.

5 Spray 9" loaf pan with cooking spray. Spoon batter into pan.

6 Bake at 350° F for 45-50 minutes.

Servings: 10

Oven Temperature: 350°F

Preparation Time: 15 minutes
Cooking Time: 50 minutes

Nutrition Facts

Serving size: 1 slice.

Amount Per Serving	
Calories	199.06
Calories From Fat (17%)	33.95
	% Daily Value
Total Fat 4.01g	6%
Saturated Fat 0.31g	2%
Cholesterol 0mg	0%
Sodium 264.3mg	11%
Potassium 381.73mg	11%
Total Carbohydrates 38.92g	13%
Fiber 3.77g	15%
Sugar 20.57g	
Protein 4.46g	9%

Herb Tahini Dressing

1 1/4	cups	water	1 1/2	tsp	dried oregano
1/2	cups	tahini	1/2	tsp	dried thyme
6		medjool dates, chopped and chopped	1	Tbs	apple cider vinegar
2	Tbs	dried basil	1/4	tsp	salt
1 1/2	tsp	rosemary			

Procedure

1 Using a blender, puree all ingredients until smooth.

Servings: 16
Yield: 16 oz

Preparation Time: 10 minutes

Nutrition Facts

Serving size: 1 oz.

Amount Per Serving	
Calories	70.07
Calories From Fat (44%)	30.66
	% Daily Value
Total Fat 3.66g	6%
Saturated Fat 0.53g	3%
Cholesterol 0mg	0%
Sodium 43.12mg	2%
Potassium 112.57mg	3%
Total Carbohydrates 9.19g	3%
Fiber 1.64g	7%
Sugar 6g	
Protein 1.65g	3%

Note

Tahini is a paste or butter made from ground sesame seeds. Tahini may be purchased at a health food store.

Sweet Dijon Mustard Dip / Dressing

2/3	cup	water
1/2	cup	tahini
4		medjool dates, pitted and chopped

1	Tbs	lemon juice
1	Tbs	Dijon mustard

Procedure

1 Using a blender, puree all ingredients until smooth.

Servings: 12
Yield: 12 oz

Nutrition Facts

Serving size: 1 oz.

Amount Per Serving	
Calories	80.4
Calories From Fat (51%)	40.75
	% Daily Value
Total Fat 4.87g	7%
Saturated Fat 0.68g	3%
Cholesterol 0mg	0%
Sodium 23.54mg	<1%
Potassium 100.16mg	3%
Total Carbohydrates 8.79g	3%
Fiber 1.5g	6%
Sugar 5.35g	
Protein 1.99g	4%

Strawberry Vinaigrette

1 cup strawberries
2   medjool dates, pitted and chopped

1 Tbs apple cider vinegar

Procedure

1 Blend until smooth.

Servings: 8
Yield: 1 cup

Nutrition Facts

Serving size: 1 oz..

Amount Per Serving	
Calories	23.09
Calories From Fat (2%)	0.55
	% Daily Value
Total Fat 0.07g	<1%
Saturated Fat 0g	0%
Cholesterol 0mg	0%
Sodium 0.34mg	<1%
Potassium 72.19mg	2%
Total Carbohydrates 5.97g	2%
Fiber 0.78g	3%
Sugar 4.92g	
Protein 0.24g	<1%

Recipe Tips

If using frozen strawberries, measure a heaping cupful then heat in microwave until warm.

Tahini Salad Dressing

1 1/4	cups	water	8		medjool dates, pitted and chopped
1/2	cup	tahini	1/2		banana, cut up
1/4	cup	lemon juice			

Procedure

1 Using a blender, puree all ingredients until smooth.

Servings: 24
Yield: 24 oz

Nutrition Facts

Serving size: 1 oz.

Amount Per Serving	
Calories	53.42
Calories From Fat (38%)	20.31
	% Daily Value
Total Fat 2.43g	4%
Saturated Fat 0.34g	2%
Cholesterol 0mg	0%
Sodium 4.2mg	<1%
Potassium 87.93mg	3%
Total Carbohydrates 8.04g	3%
Fiber 1.07g	4%
Sugar 5.68g	
Protein 1.07g	2%

Caramel Sauce

6	medjool dates, pitted and chopped		1/2 tsp	alcohol-free vanilla
3/4 cup	almond milk			

Procedure

1 Using a blender, puree all ingredients until smooth.

Servings: 12
Yield: 1 1/2 cups

Preparation Time: 10 minutes

Nutrition Facts

Serving size: 2 tablespoons.

Amount Per Serving	
Calories	36.15
Calories From Fat (5%)	1.96
	% Daily Value
Total Fat 0.24g	<1%
Saturated Fat 0g	0%
Cholesterol 0mg	0%
Sodium 11.38mg	<1%
Potassium 95.57mg	3%
Total Carbohydrates 9.13g	3%
Fiber 0.87g	3%
Sugar 7.98g	
Protein 0.28g	<1%

Recipe Tips

For a thicker sauce, reduce amount of almond milk to 1/2 cup.

Carob Tahini Sauce

1 1/2	cups	water	3/4	cup	carob powder
1/2	cup	tahini	8		medjool dates, pitted and chopped
1/4	cup	lemon juice	1		banana, cut up

Procedure

1 Using a blender, puree all ingredients until smooth.

Servings: 14
Yield: 28 oz

Preparation Time: 10 minutes

Nutrition Facts

Serving size: 2 oz..

Amount Per Serving	
Calories	135.82
Calories From Fat (26%)	34.93
	% Daily Value
Total Fat 4.17g	6%
Saturated Fat 0.59g	3%
Cholesterol 0mg	0%
Sodium 7.37mg	<1%
Potassium 165.86mg	5%
Total Carbohydrates 24.88g	8%
Fiber 6g	24%
Sugar 14.31g	
Protein 1.88g	4%

Cranberry Sauce

12 oz cranberries   1 cup   date syrup (p. 79)

Procedure

1 Mix cranberries and date syrup in medium saucepan.

2 Bring to a boil. Reduce heat and simmer for 10 minutes, stirring occasionally.

3 Cover and cool completely at room temperature. Refrigerate for several hours before serving.

Servings: 6
Yield: 1 1/2 cups

Preparation Time: 5 minutes
Cooking Time: 10 minutes

Nutrition Facts

Serving size: 1/4 cup.

Amount Per Serving	
Calories	102.65
Calories From Fat (0%)	0.3
	% Daily Value
Total Fat 0.04g	<1%
Saturated Fat 0g	0%
Cholesterol 0mg	0%
Sodium 1.74mg	<1%
Potassium 247.04mg	7%
Total Carbohydrates 27.36g	9%
Fiber 3.26g	13%
Sugar 22.44g	
Protein 0.69g	1%

Strawberry Syrup

1   heaping cup frozen strawberries
2   medjool dates, pitted and chopped

1/2   tsp   alcohol-free vanilla

Procedure

Heat strawberries in microwave until warm. Blend strawberries with dates and vanilla. Serve warm.

Servings: 2
Yield: 1 cup

Nutrition Facts

Serving size: 1/2 cup.

Amount Per Serving	
Calories	68.97
Calories From Fat (0%)	0.3
	% Daily Value
Total Fat 0.04g	<1%
Cholesterol 0mg	0%
Sodium 0.28mg	<1%
Potassium 168.07mg	5%
Total Carbohydrates 18.02g	6%
Fiber 1.61g	6%
Sugar 15.95g	
Protein 0.43g	<1%

Teriyaki Sauce

1/3	cup	soy sauce	1	tsp	minced ginger or 1/4 tsp. ground ginger
1/3	cup	water	1	Tbs	cornstarch
1/2	cup	date syrup (p. 79)	1	Tbs	water
1	clove	garlic, minced			

Procedure

1 Combine soy sauce, 1/3 cup water, date syrup, garlic and ginger into a small saucepan.

2 Bring to a boil, then reduce heat and simmer for 5 minutes.

3 Mix cornstarch with 1 T. water. Add cornstarch thickener to sauce, stirring constantly until sauce is thickened.

Servings: 6

Preparation Time: 10 minutes

Nutrition Facts

Serving size: 2 oz.

Amount Per Serving	
Calories	58.59
Calories From Fat (1%)	0.34
	% Daily Value
Total Fat 0.04g	<1%
Saturated Fat 0g	0%
Cholesterol 0mg	0%
Sodium 473.47mg	20%
Potassium 140.92mg	4%
Total Carbohydrates 14.67g	5%
Fiber 1.21g	5%
Sugar 10.92g	
Protein 1.06g	2%

Carob Fudge

12	medjool dates, pitted and chopped	1 cup	roasted almond butter
1/2 cup	carob powder	1 tsp	vanilla

Procedure

1 Mix all ingredients in food processor until well combined.

2 Spray 8" square pan with cooking spray. Spread batter into pan.

3 Refrigerate for at least two hours. Cut into 36 squares.

Servings: 36

Preparation Time: 15 minutes

Nutrition Facts

Serving size: 1 piece.

Amount Per Serving	
Calories	69.58
Calories From Fat (47%)	32.37
	% Daily Value
Total Fat 3.87g	6%
Saturated Fat 0.29g	1%
Cholesterol 0mg	0%
Sodium 0.58mg	<1%
Potassium 107.8mg	3%
Total Carbohydrates 8.43g	3%
Fiber 1.7g	7%
Sugar 6.08g	
Protein 1.6g	3%

Date Shake

3/4	cup	almond milk	1/4	cup	date syrup (p. 79)
1/2		frozen banana	2	Tbs	carob powder

Procedure

1 Using a blender, puree all ingredients until smooth.

Servings: 1
Yield: 10 oz.

Preparation Time: 5 minutes

Nutrition Facts

Serving size: Entire recipe (10.9 ounces).

Amount Per Serving	
Calories	257.51
Calories From Fat (9%)	23.36
	% Daily Value
Total Fat 2.82g	4%
Saturated Fat 0.07g	<1%
Cholesterol 0mg	0%
Sodium 137.37mg	6%
Potassium 689.22mg	20%
Total Carbohydrates 60.98g	20%
Fiber 9.28g	37%
Sugar 43.22g	
Protein 2.26g	5%

Recipe Tips

To freeze a banana: peel, cut into fourths, wrap tightly in plastic wrap and place in freezer at least overnight.
For a thicker shake, use a whole frozen banana.

Variation

For a vanilla date shake, omit carob powder and add 1 tsp. alcohol-free vanilla.

Date Spread

Serve on toast, in sandwiches, on apple slices or on celery.

6	medjool dates, pitted and chopped		1/3 cup	walnuts, chopped
1/2 cup	figs, stems removed		2 Tbs	water

Procedure

Combine all ingredients in food processor and process until smooth and mixture adheres together.

Servings: 8
Yield: 1 cup

Preparation Time: 10 minutes

Nutrition Facts

Serving size: 2 Tbs.

Amount Per Serving	
Calories	104.9
Calories From Fat (26%)	27.51
	% Daily Value
Total Fat 3.29g	5%
Saturated Fat 0.31g	2%
Cholesterol 0mg	0%
Sodium 1.32mg	<1%
Potassium 210.12mg	6%
Total Carbohydrates 20.11g	7%
Fiber 2.44g	10%
Sugar 16.55g	
Protein 1.37g	3%

Recipe Tips

If too hard from the refrigerator to spread, heat for 20-30 seconds in microwave.

Date Syrup

24	medjool dates, pitted and chopped	2	tsp	vanilla
2	cups water			

Procedure

1 Combine all ingredients and bring to a boil. Reduce heat and simmer for 15 minutes. Cool.

2 Place mixture in a blender and puree until smooth and completely blended.

3 Store in refrigerator in an air-tight container. Stir the syrup before using.

Servings: 6
Yield: 3 cups

Preparation Time: 15 minutes
Cooking Time: 15 minutes

Nutrition Facts

Serving size: 1/2 cup.

Amount Per Serving	
Calories	269.95
Calories From Fat (0%)	1.21
	% Daily Value
Total Fat 0.14g	<1%
Saturated Fat 0g	0%
Cholesterol 0mg	0%
Sodium 3.46mg	<1%
Potassium 671.02mg	19%
Total Carbohydrates 72.15g	24%
Fiber 6.43g	26%
Sugar 63.99g	
Protein 1.74g	3%

Hot Carob Drink

2	Tbs	date syrup (p. 79)		1	Tbs	carob powder
1/2	tsp	vanilla		1	cup	almond milk

Procedure

1 Combine all ingredients in mug and stir until all the carob powder has dissolved.

2 Heat in microwave for 2 minutes.

Servings: 1

Preparation Time: 5 minutes
Cooking Time: 2 minutes

Nutrition Facts

Serving size: Entire recipe (9.8 ounces).

Amount Per Serving	
Calories	133.55
Calories From Fat (22%)	28.98
	% Daily Value
Total Fat 3.5g	5%
Saturated Fat 0g	0%
Cholesterol 0mg	0%
Sodium 181.08mg	8%
Potassium 360.86mg	10%
Total Carbohydrates 25.27g	8%
Fiber 4.5g	18%
Sugar 18.27g	
Protein 1.44g	3%

Mango Chutney

2	cups	mango, peeled and chopped	2		medjool dates, pitted and chopped
1/4	cup	unsweetened apple juice	1/2	tsp	ground cinnamon
1	Tbs	apple cider vinegar	1/4	tsp	ground ginger

Procedure

1 Combine all ingredients in a medium saucepan and bring to a boil.

2 Reduce heat and simmer for 45 minutes, stirring occasionally.

Servings: 8
Yield: 2 cups

Preparation Time: 10 minutes
Cooking Time: 45 minutes

Nutrition Facts

Serving size: 1/4 cup.

Amount Per Serving	
Calories	62.4
Calories From Fat (3%)	1.57
	% Daily Value
Total Fat 0.19g	<1%
Saturated Fat 0.04g	<1%
Cholesterol 0mg	0%
Sodium 0.96mg	<1%
Potassium 162.97mg	5%
Total Carbohydrates 16.21g	5%
Fiber 1.57g	6%
Sugar 14.37g	
Protein 0.57g	1%

Recipe Tips

For spicier chutney, add 1 tsp. grated ginger root and 1 small green chile, seeded and minced.
Chutney will keep for several weeks stored in an air-tight container in the refrigerator.

Index

Printed in Great Britain
by Amazon.co.uk, Ltd.,
Marston Gate.